JESUS' PROMISE
TO THE NATIONS

JESUS' PROMISE
TO THE NATIONS

JOACHIM JEREMIAS

SCM PRESS LTD

Translated by S. H. Hooke from the German
Jesu Verheissung für die Völker
Verlag W. Kohlhammer, Stuttgart 1956, 1959

334 00780 1

First published in English 1958
by SCM Press Ltd
58 Bloomsbury Street, London WC1
Second impression, with minor revisions, 1967
Third impression 1981

Printed in Great Britain by
Richard Clay (The Chaucer Press) Ltd
Bungay, Suffolk

CONTENTS

FOREWORD

THE present work has a twofold aim. It is in the first place a New Testament study, and secondly an examination of the basis of missionary activity. Following the suggestions of Sundkler, it seeks, first of all, to draw attention to a neglected element in the message of Jesus, and attempts to show how large a place in the eschatological sayings of Jesus is given to the Old Testament conception of the pilgrimage of the nations to the Mountain of God.

At the same time the author also hopes that this work may have some significance for the inner logic of missionary activity, and for its Biblical basis. There can be no doubt that the exposition of the 'negative' element in the first part of this work, enables us to get a clear view of the immense extent of the promise which Jesus held out to the nations. The events of Easter ushered in the dawn of that final day in which the fulfilment of this promise to the nations and to Israel began to take effect. The special glory of the missionary endeavour lies in the fact that it is a very palpable part of the final consummation inaugurated at Easter.

Göttingen
New Year 1956

JOACHIM JEREMIAS

LIST OF ABBREVIATIONS

BFCT	Beiträge zur Förderung christlicher Theologie
DT	*Deutsche Theologie*
EMZ	*Evangelische Missions-Zeitschrift*
Ev. Th.	*Evangelische Theologie*
HTR	*Harvard Theological Review*
JTS	*Journal of Theological Studies*
MT	Massoretic Text
NTD	Das Neue Testament Deutsch
RHPR	*Revue d'Histoire et de Philosophie religieuses*
TB	*Theologische Blätter*
TLZ	*Theologische Literaturzeitung*
TWNT	*Theologisches Wörterbuch zum Neuen Testament*
TZ	*Theologische Zeitschrift*
ZATW	*Zeitschrift für die alttestamentliche Wissenschaft*
ZNTW	*Zeitschrift für die neutestamentliche Wissenschaft*
ZST	*Zeitschrift für systematische Theologie*
ZTK	*Zeitschrift für Theologie und Kirche*

I

THREE IMPORTANT NEGATIVE CONCLUSIONS

A. JESUS PRONOUNCES A STERN JUDGEMENT UPON THE JEWISH MISSION

AT the time of Jesus' appearance an unparalleled period of missionary activity was in progress in Israel. During its early history Israel was not a missionary people. The beginnings of missionary activity are to be found in the post-exilic period, and are closely connected with the rise and development of the Diaspora; but only after the Maccabaean period can the age of missions be strictly said to have begun.[1] This was a wholly new phenomenon: Judaism was the first great missionary religion to make its appearance in the Mediterranean world.[2]

This development reached its climax in the lifetime of Jesus and the apostles. After the destruction of the Temple in A.D. 70, and the second sack of Jerusalem in A.D. 135, the Jewish missionary activity began to decline; but there was no sudden disappearance.[3] The fatal blow to the Jewish mission, from which it never recovered, was struck by Hadrian's severe enactments, shortly before the revolt of A.D. 132, declaring circumcision to be a capital offence,[4] and thereby making conversion to Judaism practically

[1] F. M. Derwacter, *Preparing the Way for Paul, The Proselyte Movement in Later Judaism,* p. 62; B. J. Bamberger, *Proselytism in the Talmudic Period,* p. 3; cf. G. F. Moore, *Judaism in the First Three Centuries of the Christian Era* I, pp. 335 ff.

[2] G. F. Moore, op. cit. I, pp. 323 f.

[3] M. Simon, *Verus Israel, Étude sur les relations entre chrétiens et juifs dans l'empire romain (135–425),* pp. 314–55 (accurate but one-sided).

[4] A. Schlatter, *Die Tage Trajans und Hadrians* (=BFCT I 3), Gütersloh 1897, pp. 6 ff.; E. Schürer, *Geschichte des jüdischen Volkes im Zeitalter Jesu Christi* I⁴, pp. 674 ff.; Billerbeck IV, pp. 36 f.; F. M. Abel, *Histoire de la Palestine* II, Paris 1952, p. 84. Antoninus Pius (138–161) retained the decree that castration and circumcision, like murder, were capital offences, but mitigated its severity to the extent that he allowed Jews to circumcise their sons, Modestinus, *Digest.* XLVIII 8, § 11, cf. E. Schürer, op. cit. p. 677 n. 80.

impossible for a considerable time. In addition, the competition with the Christian mission rendered Jewish missionary efforts increasingly fruitless. After the recognition of Christianity as the State religion, and the renewal of anti-Jewish legislation which reached its peak in the Theodosian Code (A.D. 438), those who contemplated conversion to Judaism were faced by penalties of ever-increasing severity, even to the ultimate penalty of death.[1] In consequence the Jewish mission gradually died away. In the outlying regions of the Roman Empire up to about A.D. 1000 there were occasional cases of mass conversion to Judaism, but after that date only isolated conversions took place.[2]

Jesus thus came upon the scene in the midst of what was *par excellence* the missionary age of Jewish history. Our sources indeed are scanty, since Talmudic literature provides but little material by reason of the set-back to missionary endeavour after the destruction of the Temple in A.D. 70; nevertheless four complementary observations may give us an impression of this unique missionary period.

1. Missionary zeal was intense. In Rom. 2.17–23 Paul describes how the unshakeable certainty of the Jewish people that they possessed the revelation of the real will of God found expression in a sense of the duty incumbent upon them to make this divine will known to the heathen, to be φῶς τῶν ἐν σκότει (2.19). 'You are the lights of Israel, as the sun and the moon' says the Testament of Levi 14.3, and proceeds to affirm the duty of so living as to win the Gentiles. In Orac. Sib. III 195 f. the Jews are called 'the guide to life for all mankind'. Pursued from such a sense of duty, the mission did not confine itself to the spoken word. A comprehensive missionary literature is to be found in Hellenistic Jewry.[3] To some extent it is propaganda literature, as, for example, parts of the Sibylline Oracles (which appeal to the

---

[1] M. Simon, op. cit., pp. 338 ff.

[2] F. Goldmann, art. 'Proselyt', in *Jüdisches Lexikon* IV, Berlin 1930, col. 1149.

[3] P. Dalbert, *Die Theologie der hellenistisch-jüdischen Missionsliteratur unter Ausschluss von Philo und Josephus.* The *Book of Joseph and Asenath* should be added as a twelfth document to the eleven here discussed (see below p. 13 n. 3).

Gentiles, 'Forsake the darkness of the night, lay hold of the light,'[1] 'Be reconciled to God'[2]), or the *Book of Joseph and Asenath*[3] (where the conversion of Asenath to Judaism is described in extravagant terms); but by far the greater part of this literature is of an apologetic nature, specially designed to appeal to the educated classes, and intended to promote the success of the mission by removing the objections to Judaism and its religion.[4]

In the homeland the importance of missions is reflected in the social standing of the proselytes—for example, a long list of their names appears among the rabbinical scholars of the first century A.D.[5]—and in the efforts to improve their condition by a relaxation of religious prescriptions.[6] Moreover, light on the attitude towards missions may be gathered from Palestinian exegesis.[7] Gentiles who came into close relation with Israel, such as the Canaanite woman Shua,[8] Tamar,[9] Asenath,[10] Pharaoh's daughter who rescued Moses,[11] Jethro,[12] Rahab,[13] Ruth,[14] Ithra (in I Chron. 2.17 Jether the Ishmaelite),[15] the ship's crew in the story of Jonah,[16]

---

[1] Prooem. 27.

[2] III, 625, 628; cf. 716 ff.

[3] Ed. P. Batiffol, *Studia Patristica*, 1–2, Paris 1889–90.

[4] Above all Philo, *Apologia* (a fragment preserved in Euseb. *Praep. Evang.* VIII, 11); Josephus, *Con. Ap.* I, II. But the historical writings of Hellenistic Jews such as Demetrius, Eupolemus, Artapanus, *et al.*, the philosophical works of Aristobulus and Philo, as well as the pseudonymous Hellenistic-Jewish literature (such as Ps.-Hecataeus and Ps.-Aristeas), also exhibit extensive apologetic tendencies, cf. O. Stählin, *Die hellenistisch-jüdische Literatur*, offprint from W. von Christ's *Griechische Literaturgeschichte* II 1⁶, Munich 1921, pp. 588–624; P. Dalbert, op. cit.

[5] J. Jeremias, *Jerusalem zur Zeit Jesu* IIB, p. 103 = ³1962, p. 267.

[6] An authoritative account of these efforts is the subject of W. G. Braude's book, *Jewish Proselyting in the First Five Centuries of the Common Era*.

[7] B. J. Bamberger, *Proselytism in the Talmudic Period*, pp. 174–217.

[8] Gen. 38.2: Targ. Jerus. I to Gen. 38.2.

[9] Gen. 38.6: Philo, *De virtutibus* 221.

[10] Gen. 41.50: *Joseph and Asenath*.

[11] Ex. 2.5: b.Meg. 13a; b.Sota 12b.

[12] Ex. 18.5 f.: Targ. Jerus. I to Ex. 18.6; Mekh. Ex. 18.6. Cf. B. J. Bamberger, op. cit. pp. 182–191.

[13] Josh. 2.1–21: Mekh. Ex. 18.1; Midr. Ruth 1.16 f. Further examples in Billerbeck I, p. 21.

[14] Midr. Koh. 8.10.

[15] II Sam. 17.25: Midr. Ruth 1.21.

[16] Jonah 1.16: end of Tanch. *wayyiqra* (ed. Vienna 1863, p. 138a).

even the 'mixed multitude' that accompanied Israel on the wilderness journey,[1] are regarded as proselytes; Isaac,[2] Jacob,[3] Judah,[4] Joseph,[5] Moses,[6] Jethro,[7] Boaz,[8] are missionaries. Similarly, Solomon's harem becomes evidence for his successful missionary activity.[9] Above all Abraham is hailed as a missionary: himself the first proselyte,[10] he won over a host of Gentiles to belief in the one God,[11] while Sarah converted the women.[12] So successful was he as a missionary, that he was said to have been the first to cause God, who hitherto had only been known as the King of heaven, to be recognized as the King of heaven and earth.[13] Thus the 'Father of the Proselytes'[14] becomes the brilliant prototype of the Missionary: 'Cause him (God) to be adored by all creatures, as your Father Abraham did.'[15] Moreover, significant light on missionary modes of thought is thrown by the fact that the term Diaspora lost its ill-omened connotation;[16] Israel's dispersion among the Gentiles was no longer regarded as God's judgement, but came to be seen as a divinely-given opportunity to glorify him among the Gentiles.[17]

2. In the Hellenistic world Jewish missionary zeal encountered

[1]Num. 11.4: Targ. Jerus. I to Num. 11.4.
[2]Gen. R. 84 to Gen. 37.1.
[3]Ibid.
[4]Targ. Jerus. I to Gen. 38.2.
[5]Gen. R. 90 to Gen. 41.55; 91 to 42.6.
[6]Midr. Koh. 8.10.
[7]Mekh. Ex. 18.27.
[8]Midr. Koh. 8.10.
[9]j. San. II, 20c. 24 f.; Num. R. 10 to Num. 6.2.
[10]Mekh. Ex. 22.20; b. Sukk. 49b; cf. Rom. 4.11.
[11]Gen. R. 39 to Gen. 12.8; 48 to Gen. 18.1; 84 to Gen. 37.1; Siphre Deut. 32 to Deut. 6.5 *et al.*; cf. Billerbeck III, pp. 195 f., 215.
[12]Gen. R. 39 to Gen. 12.5; 84 to Gen. 37.1.
[13]Siphre Deut. 313 to Deut. 32.10. Interpretation of the words in Gen. 14.19 'Blessed be Abraham of the Most High God, creator of heaven and earth', has been carried so far as to ascribe to Abraham the epithet 'Creator of heaven and earth'. Conversion to Judaism means a new creation, hence, as a missionary, Abraham is 'the companion of the Creator of the world' (Gen. R. 43 to Gen. 14.19).
[14]Tanch. to Gen. 14.1 (ed. S. Buber, Wilna 1885, p. 32a. 27).
[15]Siphre Deut. 32 to Deut. 6.5.
[16]Cf. W. C. van Unnik in: *Het oudste Christendom en de antieke cultuur,* edited by J. H. Waszink, W. C. van Unnik and Ch. de Beus, Vol. I, Haarlem 1951.
[17]Tobit 13.3–6; b. Pes. 87b. Later instances in Braude, *Jewish Proselyting in the First Five Centuries,* pp. 18 f.

a wave of deeper religious longing. Widespread, indeed, within the disillusioned and decadent world of antiquity was the belief that the East was the source of true religion. In the form of Judaism with its biblical monotheism and its aniconic cult, polytheism was confronted with a relentless criticism and an exclusive claim. It heard a message of revealed truth enshrined in inspired Scriptures, rigidly intolerant of any attempt at syncretism.[1] Such a message demanded conversion in view of an imminent divine judgement, and was inseparably bound up with a strict ethical code. In short, it offered a form of divine worship towering far above all contemporary cults and systems of religion. The strength of the impact of this superiority may be gauged by the fact that the Jewish mission achieved its remarkable success in the face of the widely diffused anti-Semitism of the ancient world.[2]

3. The Jewish mission made every possible effort to facilitate the passage of Gentiles from heathenism. The proclamation of Judaism was simplified by the relegation of the ritual prescriptions to the background and by emphasis on the moral code;[3] moreover, the Jewish religion was presented to the Gentile in a religio-philosophic dress.[4] It had become clear that the greatest obstacle to the conversion of Gentiles was the demand that they should be circumcised; the difficulty was met by the creation everywhere of a circle of 'godfearers' loosely connected with the synagogues, from whom, beyond the recognition of the one God, nothing was required save the keeping of the most important commandments (i.e. observance of the sabbath and the food laws).[5] Experience showed that the next generation frequently

---

[1] The Synagogue should not be held responsible for the occasional cases of Jewish-Gentile syncretism, especially occurring in Asia Minor.

[2] E. Schürer, *Geschichte des jüdischen Volkes* III⁴, pp. 150–5; J. Leipoldt, *Antisemitismus in der alten Welt,* Leipzig 1933; the same author's art. 'Antisemitismus' in *Reallexikon für Antike und Christentum* I, Stuttgart 1950, col. 469–76.

[3] b. Shab. 31a: for the benefit of a Gentile who wished to become a convert, Hillel summed up the whole Torah in a single sentence: 'What you would not have done to yourself, that do not to your neighbour—that is the whole Torah, the rest is commentary; go and learn.'

[4] Philo especially.

[5] E. Schürer, op. cit. III, p. 175.

advanced to full conversion by the acceptance of circumcision.[1]

4. The success of the mission was extraordinary. We learn from the book of Acts how everywhere the Christian missionaries found proselytes and godfearers. These were to be found in Jerusalem[2] as much as in Caesarea;[3] in Syria,[4] Asia Minor,[5] Greece,[6] and in Rome[7] as much as in Egypt[8] and in Parthia.[9] Women predominated: in Damascus, according to Josephus, almost the entire female population had joined the synagogue;[10] in Rome, Nero's consort, Poppaea Sabina, was a θεοσεβής.[11] The overwhelming success of the mission of the apostle Paul, who in the space of ten years had established centres of the Christian faith throughout almost the whole of the contemporary world, depended partly on the fact that everywhere he was able to build on ground prepared by the Jewish mission.

Of course the Jewish mission had its limitations, and should not be compared with what we understand by the term 'mission' today. We know absolutely nothing about any official sending forth of missionaries by the Jewish authorities;[12] rather did the mission in general depend *upon personal initiative* (cf. John 7.35) and upon the attraction of synagogue worship. The Diaspora constituted the primary channel of the mission, a fact which is attested by its abundant missionary literature; whereas in the homeland there was to some extent a tendency to adopt a passive

---

[1] Juvenal, *Sat.* 14.96–106.

[2] Acts 6.5.

[3] 10.2.

[4] 6.5.

[5] 13.16, 26, 43, 50.

[6] 16.14; 17.4, 17; 18.7.

[7] Josephus, *Ant.* XVIII, 82. Roman inscriptions in J.-B. Frey, *Corpus Inscriptionum Iudaicarum* I, Rome 1936, no. 21, pp. 19 f. (on the subject see J. Jeremias, *Infant Baptism in the First Four Centuries*, London 1960, p. 47 n. 1); no. 68, pp. 40 f.; 202, p. 141; 222, pp. 158 f.; 256, pp. 181 f.; 462, pp. 340 f.; 523, pp. 383 f.

[8] Josephus, *Ant.* XIV, 116; Tos. Qid. V, 4.

[9] Josephus, *Ant.* XX, 17 ff. *et al.*

[10] Josephus, *Bell.* II, 560.

[11] Josephus, *Ant.* XX, 195, cf. *Vita* 16. θεοσεβής is evidently not a general term of appreciation, but indicates a favourable attitude towards Judaism. Cf. G. Bertram, *TWNT* III, p. 126 n. 16.

[12] W. G. Braude, *Jewish Proselyting in the First Five Centuries*, p. 5.

attitude of waiting for the Gentiles to come forward (hence the term προσήλυτος meaning 'he who comes forward'). Indeed, the theologians of the school of Shammai were sceptical with regard to proselytes.[1] Shammai's rival, Hillel (*circa* A.D. 20), was certainly favourable to missions;[2] one of his sayings was, 'love mankind and bring them to the Law'.[3] The immediate future was destined to follow Hillel's theology. But the most obvious defect of the Jewish mission lay in its insistence on the inseparable connexion between religion and national custom. Conversion to the Jewish religion meant nothing less than naturalization, becoming a Jew: the Jewish mission was at the same time national propaganda. Obvious as are these limitations, they in no way minimize the significance of the fact that Jesus grew up in the midst of a people actively engaged, both by the spoken and the written word, in a Gentile mission, whose impelling motive was a profound sense of their obligation to glorify their God in the Gentile world.

With this fact in mind, it becomes all the more strange to realize that the only utterance of Jesus which refers to the Jewish mission should be an incisive criticism: 'Woe unto you, scribes and Pharisees, hypocrites! for ye compass sea and land to make one proselyte; and when he is become so, ye make him twofold more a son of Gehenna than yourselves' (Matt. 23.15). The logion has its source in an old Aramaic tradition.[4] It recognizes in its first half

[1]Shammai rejected applicants, b. Shab. 31a; the Shammaite R. Eliezer b. Hyrcanus was pessimistic about proselytes, Mekh. Exod. 22.20; 23.4, cf. W. Bacher, *Die Agada der Tannaiten* I², Strasbourg 1903, pp. 106 f. B. J. Bamberger's criticism (in *Proselytism in the Talmudic Period*, pp. 278, 280–2) is not convincing. It is true that the Shammaites imputed a lesser degree of uncleanness to Gentiles than did the followers of Hillel (Pes. 8.8; Eduy. 5.2); but this was on account of their conservatism, and not from any love for missions (Billerbeck I, p. 104). (Similarly the ruling of the school of Hillel which attributed to Gentiles the same degree of uncleanness as that caused by contact with a corpse, had no relation to their attitude towards the Gentile mission; but was simply aimed at preventing the prevalence of mixed marriages between Jews and Gentiles.)

[2]b. Shab. 31a.

[3]Pirqe Ab. 1.12.

[4]Semitisms are: (*a*) the paratactic sentence-structure, which makes it seem as if the woe were pronounced against the 'compassing sea and land' as well, whereas it only refers to the final words. The woe was not uttered against the scribes and Pharisees because of their missionary zeal, but because they made

the zeal which did not shrink from dangerous journeys by land and sea in the interests of the mission, but proceeds to draw from it the damning conclusion that the only result of the mission was so to corrupt the converted Gentiles that they became children of the devil more wicked than those who had converted them.[1] It

their converts children of hell. (*b*) The change from ὅτι in v. 15 to οἱ in v. 16 after οὐαί points to an underlying Aramaic דֵּי· (*c*) It is only very rarely that οὐαί occurs in the *Koiné* (Arrian, *Epictetus* 3.19.1; 3.22.32; Pap. Oxyrh. 413. 184 f.) as a Latinism (= *vae*), while it is common in the LXX and the N.T. Here οὐαί is not a transcription of the Heb. הוֹי or אוֹי (so Blass-Debrunner §4. 2a), but is an exact reproduction of the Aramaic וָי ; hence in Matt. 23.15 it is not a Septuagintism (so Blass-Debrunner), but an Aramaism. (*d*) The contrasted pair ἡ θάλασσα καὶ ἡ ξηρά (γῆ) is not found in Greek, but, on the other hand, it is common in the O.T. (Gen. 1.10; Jonah 1.9, 13; Ps. 66.6) and in Rabbinic literature (examples are given in A. Schlatter, *Der Evangelist Matthäus*, Stuttgart 1929, p. 674). (*e*) Probably ἕνα also is a Semitism. It could be a literal translation of the indefinite Aramaic חַד (J. Jeremias, *The Parables of Jesus*[2], London 1963, p. 200 n. 38), hence it should not be stressed in translation. (*f*) Finally, a more obvious Semitism is to be seen in υἱὸς γεέννης. The term 'sons of hell' (בְּנֵי גֵיהִנֹּם b. Rosh Hashana 17a) was used to designate those who had deserved the punishment of hell.

[1] J. Munck, *Paul and the Salvation of Mankind*, London 1959, pp. 265–267, attempts to avoid the conclusion that Matt. 23.15 is evidence of a vigorous Jewish missionary activity. He offers two possibilities of doing so: 1. That Matt. 23.15 is not an authentic saying of Jesus, but comes from the period after the beginning of the Gentile mission and relates to a particular historical situation, namely, to the concourse of rulers in A.D. 43. At that time Herod Agrippa I invited five Roman vassal-princes to Tiberias (Jos. *Ant.* XIX, 338–41), including Antiochus IV of Commagene. Josephus later reports that the son of Antiochus IV, Epiphanes, had promised Agrippa I to adopt the Jewish religion and to marry Agrippa's sister Drusilla (Jos. *Ant.* XX, 139); hence Munck conjectures that this undertaking may have been given at the meeting of the princes, which is quite possible. He thus regards the Commagenian prince Epiphanes as the 'one proselyte' of Matt. 23.15, and makes the further suggestion that Agrippa I was accompanied by a staff of scribes and Pharisees at Tiberias to convert Epiphanes, a much harder supposition to accept. Apart from the late dating of the saying and its precarious dependence upon a single incident, linguistic considerations are against this interpretation of Matt. 23.15; in view of what has been said above in n. 4 under (*e*) it is questionable whether it is permissible to translate ἕνα προσήλυτον as 'a single proselyte'; moreover, the journey from Jerusalem to Tiberias can hardly be described as 'compassing sea and land'. 2. As a second way of avoiding the interpretation of Matt. 23.15 as a reference to a vigorous proselytizing activity, Munck suggests that the term προσήλυτος may refer to Jewish adherents of the Pharisaic party. The Pharisees 'hunt' for pupils (p. 267). But προσήλυτος never has this connotation. It always refers to Gentile converts to Judaism. Hence we must adhere to the interpretation which we have given in the text.

may be admitted that Jesus was condemning a superficial proselytizing,[1] that his saying was aimed at the smug self-righteousness
of the Pharisees and the fanaticism of their converts,[2] and that his
woe could hardly have been pronounced against the Gentile
mission itself; nevertheless the riddle still remains why this harsh
saying about converts who became children of the devil should be
the only utterance of Jesus which we possess concerning the
Jewish mission, and that in an age of missionary activity unparalleled in Jewish history.

B. JESUS FORBADE HIS DISCIPLES DURING HIS LIFETIME TO PREACH TO NON-JEWS

Our perplexity increases when we read the instructions which
Jesus gave to his disciples:

> 'Go not to[3] the Gentiles,[4]
>
> and enter not the province[5] of Samaria;

---

[1]Critical utterances of the Rabbis concerning proselytes are discussed by
W. G. Braude, *Jewish Proselyting in the First Five Centuries*, pp. 39–48.

[2]Cf. Acts 13.50.

[3]Εἰς ὁδόν = Aram. לְאוֹרַח? 'in the direction of', 'towards', 'to'. Cf. Targ.
on I Kings 18.43; Ezek. 8.5; 40.44. Hence the rendering 'into any way' is
erroneous.

[4]That the term ἔθνη has a special biblical connotation is shown by the way
in which ἔθνη and Samaritans are contrasted with Israel; it is a collective term
with a religious connotation denoting Gentiles in contrast with the chosen
people (cf. K. L. Schmidt, *TWNT* II, pp. 362 ff.).

[5]The singular εἰς πόλιν Σαμαριτῶν is particularly striking, as is also the
absence of the article before πόλιν. What is the meaning of 'Enter not into
any city of the Samaritans'? Is Jesus only forbidding the disciples to
visit Samaritan cities in contrast to Samaritan villages? Or is he only forbidding them to enter the capital Samaria? In the latter case the article should
stand before πόλιν. But all the difficulties disappear when we recognize that
πόλιν in our passage is an erroneous rendering of the Aramaic מְדִינָא, which
in Palestinian Aramaic means (a) in the indeterminate state מְדִינָא? 'province',
and in the determinate state מְדִינְתָּא? 'city' (G. Dalman, *Aramäisch-neuhe-
bräisches Handwörterbuch*[2], Frankfort 1922, p. 225; C. C. Torrey in *HTR* 17,
1924, pp. 83 ff.; H. Grimme in *Bibl. Ztschr.* 23, 1935–6, p. 253; H. Sahlin,
Der Messias und das Gottesvolk (= Acta Semin. Neotest. Upsal. 12), Uppsala
1945, pp. 141 f.; M. Black, *An Aramaic Approach to the Gospels and Acts*[2],
Oxford 1954, p. 11). Hence the construct state מְדִינַת which may be assumed
to underlie Matt. 10.5 is capable of two renderings: it had the meaning 'province', and was incorrectly rendered by πόλις. The same erroneous rendering

but go rather to[1] the lost sheep of the house of Israel'[2]

(Matt. 10.5 f.)

It is hardly accidental that this tristich,[3] based on Aramaic tradition, has no parallel in Mark or Luke; it strictly prohibits the disciples from undertaking the Gentile mission. By the instruction not to go to Samaria the south is closed to them, while the command not to go to the Gentiles cuts them off from the other three points of the compass: hence they are limited to Galilee. An attempt has been made to temper the severity of this saying to some extent by suggesting that it applied only to the first sending out of the disciples. But this loophole is closed by the saying in Matt. 10.23: 'When they persecute you in this city[4] flee into the[5] next: for verily I say unto you,[6] Ye shall not have gone through the cities of Israel, till the Son of man be come'. For this early ἀμήν-saying, whose antiquity is attested both by its incompatibility with Matthew's universalistic outlook,[7] and by the dismay which it must have caused as an unfulfilled prediction, indicates that the proclamation of the message in Israel would not be terminated even at the parousia.[8]

---

of מְדִינָא by πόλις occurs also in Luke 1.39 and in Acts 8.5, cf. also Luke 8.39 (καθ' ὅλην τὴν πόλιν='province') with the parallel in Mark 5.20 (ἐν τῇ Δεκαπόλει). That Matt. 10.5 f. is the translation of an original Semitic text is established by the absence of the article before πόλιν, which points to an underlying construct state.

[1]See below p. 26 n. 2 under (c): πρός is a translation variant.

[2]οἶκος in the sense of 'tribe', 'lineage', 'community' is a Semitism. The absence of the article before οἴκου Ἰσραήλ again points to an underlying construct state.

[3]The structure is Palestinian: two three-beat lines in synthetic parallelism are followed by a final line in antithetic parallelism.

[4]Ἐν τῇ πόλει ταύτῃ: the superfluous translation of the demonstrative is a Semitism. Cf. J. Jeremias, *The Eucharistic Words of Jesus*[2], London 1966, pp. 183 f.

[5]Εἰς τὴν ἑτέραν: the definite article must be an Aramaism.

[6]On the ἀμήν-words cf. J. Jeremias, 'Characteristics of the *ipsissima vox Jesu*', in J. Jeremias, *The Prayers of Jesus*, London 1967, pp. 108–115.

[7]See below pp. 24 f., 34 f.

[8]It is very doubtful whether Matt. 7.6 is also to be interpreted as forbidding the Gentile mission (T. W. Manson, *Jesus and the Non-Jews*, p. 3, puts forward this suggestion). Most probably 'dogs' and 'swine' should be understood to mean, in the sense of II Peter 2.22, those who have wholly abandoned themselves to vicious courses.

Confirmation of the mission of the disciples to Israel is afforded by the fact that they were twelve in number,[1] clearly giving expression to the fact that the demand of Jesus was addressed to a nation composed of twelve tribes. Yet it must not be overlooked that the twelvefold aspect of the disciples envisages, not the contemporary Israel, but the eschatological people of God. This may be inferred, not only from the eschatological function assigned to the disciples (Matt. 19.28 par. Luke ¯22.29 f.), but also from the number twelve itself: the Jewish nation of that time embraced only two and a half tribes;[2] hence the number twelve includes also the nine and a half lost tribes of the northern kingdom,[3] whose restoration formed part of the final expectation. Thus the twelve disciples are the representatives of the people of God in the ultimate restoration, of the extent of whose kingdom more will be said later.

Now it is apparent that in contrast to these two sayings limiting the mission of the disciples to Israel, which belong to Matthew's special material, we find a series of pre-resurrection sayings of Jesus which envisage a mission of the disciples to the Gentiles. But, with regard to these pre-resurrection mission-sayings, probably without exception, the question arises whether they are not otherwise to be understood, or whether they represent distortions and expansions of the sayings of Jesus.

[1] On the historicity of the circle of the Twelve see J. Jeremias, *Jesus als Weltvollender* (=BFCT XXXIII 4), Gütersloh 1930, p. 71 n. 4; K. H. Rengstorf, *TWNT* II, pp. 325 f.

[2] The attempt of G. H. Box in *The Ezra-Apocalypse*, London 1912, p. 296, to explain the number 2½ with the help of Josh. 22.9, is very artificial: he suggests that the number has been erroneously inferred from a reference of the passage to the two and a half transjordanic tribes (Reuben, Gad and the half-tribe of Manasseh) in Josh. 22.9. But the fact that the two and a half or three tribes, Judah, Benjamin and Levi, are in question, has been conclusively established from the evidence of the genealogical material of the post-exilic period (J. Jeremias, *Jerusalem zur Zeit Jesu* IIB, pp. 93, 149 = [3]1962, pp. 257, 312); also from the Hebrew Testament of Naphtali, 3, and from IQM 1.2; 3.14; 4.15.

[3] Syr. Bar. 62.5; 77.19; 78.1; IV Esd. 13.40(syr. arab.); Asc. Isa. 3.2; Commodian (4th cent.), *Carm. Apol.*, 936–9. Along with the number 9½, the numbers 10, and occasionally 9, have found currency.

Beginning with Mark as the earliest of the Synoptists, we find only[1] two closely connected passages: 13.10 and 14.9. The words of the early Aramaic logion[2] in Mark 14.9 (par. Matt. 26.13) ὅπου ἐὰν κηρυχθῇ τὸ εὐαγγέλιον εἰς ὅλον τὸν κόσμον, one of the thirteen ἀμήν-sayings in Mark,[3] seem to presuppose a worldwide mission which would celebrate the act of the unnamed woman throughout the world; there can be no doubt that this is how Mark and Matthew understood the saying. But it is questionable whether this was the original meaning of the saying. I have attempted to show elsewhere[4] that the ὅπου-phrase is an interpretation and that εὐαγγέλιον is used in the early pre-Pauline sense of Rev. 14.6 f., where, in the hour of final fulfilment, an angelic voice proclaims 'the everlasting gospel of triumph'. Such an interpretation would give a strong eschatological colouring to Mark 14.9: 'Amen, I say unto you, (when[5] the triumphal news is proclaimed [by God's angel] to all the world), her act will be remembered (before God), so that he may be gracious to her (at the last judgement).' Hence we are to understand that 'the proclamation to all the world' will not be by men in the time before the Parousia, but by God's angel at the last day. If this is the correct meaning of the saying, then it did not originally refer to a worldwide mission of the disciples, but to the final fulfilment and the last judgement. In which case a similar interpretation should be given to the closely-related isolated saying in Mark 13.10[6] which

---

[1]Mark 5.19 (ὕπαγε εἰς τὸν οἶκόν σου πρὸς τοὺς σούς, καὶ ἀπάγγειλον αὐτοῖς κτλ.) is hardly in place here. The injunction to the man who had been healed to tell 'his own' what God had done for him, would seem primarily to refer to his family; cf. the parallel in Luke 8.39.

[2]Besides (a) ἀμὴν δὲ λέγω ὑμῖν, (b) κηρυχθῇ εἰς = Aramaic בְּשֵׂר לְ ? followed by the indication of the individual or the group to whom the message refers (examples are given in *ZNTW* 44, 1952-3, p. 103 n. 7; in Old Testament Hebrew, on the other hand, בְּשֵׂר is construed with accus. of the person), and (c) the twice repeated circumlocution for the divine activity by the use of the passive (κηρυχθῇ, λαληθήσεται), are Semitisms.

[3]On these cf. the study mentioned above, p. 20 n. 6.

[4]'Markus 14, 9', in J. Jeremias, *Abba*, Göttingen 1966, pp. 115–20.

[5]Ὅπου ἐάν refers to a single occurrence, as in Mark 14.14a.

[6]That Mark 13.10 was originally transmitted as an isolated logion is evident from the fact that it breaks the connexion between vv. 9 and 11; also it is absent from the parallels in Matt. 10.17–22; Luke 12.11 f. The verse has

read in its original[1] Matthaean form:[2] 'And this[3] gospel of the
kingdom shall be preached[4] in the whole world for a testimony
unto all the nations; and then shall the end come' (Matt. 24.14).
Here, too, the original reference is not to human proclamation, but
to an apocalyptic event, namely, the angelic proclamation of God's
final act (cf. Rev. 14.6 f.).[5]

---

possibly been added *ad vocem* εἰς μαρτύριον (Mark 13.9) in the Marcan context; this change is wanting in Mark 13.10 but is found in the Matthaean form
of this verse (Matt. 24.14).

[1]That Matt. 24.14 has the older form of the logion may be inferred from
the absence of πρῶτον; for in Mark 7.27 πρῶτον is secondary; cf. p. 29 n. 2.

[2]Further, the words εἰς μαρτύριον, which are wanting in Mark 13.10, are
possibly evidence for the antiquity of the Matthaean form (see p. 22 n. 6).
On the other hand the genitive τῆς βασιλείας in Matt. 24.14 is apparently
secondary in contrast with Mark 13.10; 14.9; Matt. 26.13. Besides, comparison with the fore-mentioned passages suggests the possibility that the
two phrases ἐν ὅλῃ τῇ οἰκουμένῃ and εἰς μαρτύριον πᾶσιν τοῖς ἔθνεσιν (Matt.
24.14) represent alternative (or expanded) renderings of one and the same
original Semitic text.

[3]τοῦτο is a superfluous demonstrative, wanting in Mark 13.10 (see above
p. 20 n. 4).

[4]On בְּשַׂר ? with following indication of the individual, see above p. 22
n. 2; the εἰς in Mark 13.10; 14.9 is more original than ἐν in Matt. 24.14;
26.13.

[5]The same conclusion, namely, that Mark 13.10 and 14.9 did not originally
contemplate a Gentile mission, is arrived at by an entirely different route by
G. D. Kilpatrick in 'The Gentile Mission in Mark and Mark 13.9–11', in
Studies in the Gospels. Essays in Memory of R. H. Lightfoot, pp. 145–58. Kilpatrick
does not regard Mark 13.10 as an independent clause. He prefers, with
Burkitt, to connect the beginning of Mark 13.10, καὶ εἰς πάντα τὰ ἔθνη, with
v. 9, and therefore regards the εἰς in the beginning of v. 10, with Turner, as a
preposition indicating place: the disciples will be brought before Jewish and
Gentile authorities, 'for a testimony to them and among all nations (because
the end is near)'. He links the remaining words of Mark 13.10 (πρῶτον δεῖ
κηρυχθῆναι τὸ εὐαγγέλιον) directly with v. 11, 'first (before they arrest you)
must the gospel be preached, and when they bring you before the authorities,
do not be careful . . .'. Thus v. 10b merely says that the preaching is the
occasion for the arrest. Similarly Kilpatrick regards the εἰς in Mark 14.9 as a
preposition of place ('throughout the whole world'). According to Kilpatrick there is nothing in either of the passages which suggests that the
preaching there (Mark 13.10 and 14.9) mentioned will be directed towards any
other audience than the Jews in Palestine and the Diaspora. Kilpatrick's conclusion, 'with these two verses our clearest references to preaching to Gentiles
disappear from Mark' (p. 149), agrees with mine, although, as I have said,
arrived at by another route. On the other hand, in view of what is said on
p. 33 and in Part III of the present work, the sweeping generalization 'uni-
versalism is absent from Mark' (p. 157) cannot be sustained.

The following passages, apart from the two verses 24.14; 26.13, mentioned above, occur in Matthew, in which a reference to the Gentile mission of the disciples may be recognized: 5.13: ὑμεῖς ἐστε τὸ ἅλας τῆς γῆς (absent from the parallel passages in Mark 9.50; Luke 14.34); 5.14: ὑμεῖς ἐστε τὸ φῶς τοῦ κόσμου (likewise only in Matt.; an established formula which here has an eschatological significance, cf. Billerbeck I, pp. 237 f., and see below p. 66); 10.18: εἰς μαρτύριον αὐτοῖς καὶ τοῖς ἔθνεσιν (the last three words are missing from the parallels in Mark 13.9; Luke 21.12); 21.43 (likewise missing from the Marcan and Lucan parallels); in 22.9 f. Matt. is probably thinking of the Gentiles, where the original reference was to the publicans and sinners; perhaps also in 25.40 he intended the words ἑνὶ τούτων τῶν ἀδελφῶν μου τῶν ἐλαχίστων to refer to the disciples who were preaching to the Gentiles (but the τούτων is a superfluous demonstrative, cf. p. 20 n. 4; this implies that the original reference was to all the poor and needy). Thus in every passage we have to do with reinterpretations or additions of the evangelist.[1]

The only occurrences in Luke are the sending-out of the Seventy (10.1, a secondary doublet of 9.1), and the second invitation in 14.23 (the parallel in Matt. 22.1–10 has only one invitation to the unbidden guests).

The fact that Jesus, during his lifetime, sent his disciples to Israel alone, is confirmed by the behaviour of the primitive church, although here caution is necessary in drawing conclusions.

The most important passage is Gal. 2.7 f., which says of Peter that he was entrusted with τὸ εὐαγγέλιον (or ἡ ἀποστολή v. 8) τῆς περιτομῆς. The point is disputed whether the genitive τῆς περιτομῆς is to be understood ethnographically (preaching only to the Jews), geographically (preaching only in Palestine), or with reference to the content of the message (preaching the observance of the law). In any case it indicates a fundamental limitation of Peter's mission to the sphere of Jewry. It is true that James, Cephas, and John recognize Paul's call to preach to those who are not under the law;

[1]On the missionary commission in Matt. 28.18–20, which does not belong to the pre-resurrection sayings, see below pp. 38 f.

nevertheless they are aware that they themselves have been sent εἰς τὴν περιτομήν (2.9).

The same situation is reflected in the story of Cornelius (Acts 10.1–11. 18). Peter baptizes the Gentile Cornelius only as the consequence of an unmistakable divine revelation (10.44–48),[1] and then has to encounter a storm of indignation in Jerusalem (11.1–3). Now it must not be assumed out of hand that this indignation was aroused merely by the fact that Peter had baptized a Gentile, for the proselyte Nicolas, 6.5, was already a member of the Jerusalem community; it arose rather from the circumstance that Peter had baptized Cornelius without first having had him circumcised (11.3, cf. 15.1, 5).

Hence it is wrong to say that the primitive community at Jerusalem was fundamentally opposed to the admission of Gentiles;[2] according to Acts 11 they had only objected to Gentiles being freed from the obligation to be circumcised and to keep the law. Nevertheless it remains a striking fact that we have no support for the view that the early church embarked upon the Gentile mission immediately after the resurrection (cf. especially Acts 11.19). It is more probable that, with the exception of such isolated instances as Acts 10.1 ff., those who began and continued the Gentile mission were the Hellenistic members of the primitive community who were driven out after the persecution following Stephen's death (8.25 ff.; 11.20 ff.; cf. also 8.4 ff.), until Paul arose as the declared apostle of the Gentiles. This state of affairs makes it improbable that the activity of the disciples during Jesus' lifetime was directed towards the Gentiles.

C. JESUS LIMITED HIS OWN ACTIVITY TO ISRAEL

The problem which confronts us at the present stage of our

---

[1] God fulfils the promise that he will pour out his Spirit upon 'all flesh' (Joel 3.1 = Acts 2.17), and announces that he is including the Gentiles also in the redeemed community.

[2] We agree with E. Lohmeyer's words in 'Mir ist gegeben alle Gewalt!', in *In Memoriam Ernst Lohmeyer*, p. 43: 'The fundamental legitimacy of the Gentile mission' 'remained unassailable from the outset', except that it is preferable to speak of the 'reception of the Gentiles', rather than of the 'Gentile mission'.

inquiry, becomes increasingly urgent when we turn to the activity of Jesus himself.

Even without overstepping the boundaries of Palestine, Jesus must often have come into contact with non-Jews. Although Gentiles may have been comparatively scarce in the hill-country of Galilee, they were much more numerous about the Lake of Gennesaret, and still more so in Jerusalem. The question of whether he should direct his activity towards the Gentiles cannot have been avoided by Jesus.

The attitude, indeed, which Jesus adopted towards this question was one of definite refusal: οὐκ ἀπεστάλην εἰ μὴ εἰς τὰ πρόβατα τὰ ἀπολωλότα οἴκου Ἰσραήλ, are the words of an isolated logion,[1] which goes back to an early Aramaic tradition (Matt. 15.24).[2] Jesus expressly rejected the idea that he was also sent to the Gentiles; his mission was confined to the lost sheep of the Israelite community.[3] The passive ἀπεστάλην contains the veiled implica-

---

[1] It is absent from the Marcan parallel (Mark 7.25), and reappears in Matt. 10.6, which is peculiar to Matthew, as an injunction to the disciples.

[2] (a) οὐκ . . . εἰ μή = אִלָּא . . . לֹא = only. (b) The passive ἀπεστάλην is a circumlocution for the divine activity (K. H. Rengstorf, *TWNT* I, p. 402 n. 34). (c) Ἀποστέλλειν εἰς followed by indication of the circle concerned, to whom anyone is sent, is not found in classical Greek, but occurs in LXX Greek, Jer. 30.8 (MT 49.14); III Kings 18.20; Acts 26.17 (cf. ἐξαποστέλλειν εἰς LXX Judg. 19.29 A; Obad. 1; Acts 22.21); εἰς is a rendering of the Hebrew בְּ . If therefore it is probable that ἀποστέλλειν εἰς τινα should be regarded as a Semitism, this conclusion is confirmed by the comparison of our passage with Matt. 10.6, πορεύεσθε δὲ μᾶλλον πρὸς τὰ πρόβατα τὰ ἀπολωλότα οἴκου Ἰσραήλ. For the second halves of Matt. 15.24 and 10.6 agree verbally, except for a difference in the prepositions (Matt. 15.24 has εἰς, 10.6 has πρός). This interchange of εἰς and πρός is to be regarded as a translation variant. (Moreover it should be remarked with regard to ἀποστέλλειν εἰς τινα, that Matt. 15.24 is pre-Matthaean translation Greek, for elsewhere Matthew always has ἀποστέλλειν πρός τινα: 21.34, 37; 23.34, 37; 27.19.) (d) On οἴκου Ἰσραήλ cf. p. 20 n. 2.

[3] The genitive οἴκου Ἰσραήλ can be a partitive genitive (in which case the mission of Jesus is limited to a part of Israel, namely, to the lost ones of Israel), or an explanatory genitive (in which case Jesus is saying that he has been sent to the whole of Israel in its lost condition). Old Testament usage (Jer. 50.6; Ezek. 34.5 ff.; Isa. 53.6) supports the second of these two interpretations of the genitive, as do also the contrasts in the context of Matt. 10.6 and 15.24: Gentiles and Samaritans contrasted with Israel, and Gentiles with Israel. Thus Jesus thought of the whole of Israel as a lost and shepherdless flock, including even the religious people, than whom none were more lost (cf. Luke 15.25 ff.).

tion that this is doubtless the will of God. The Scripture says:
'And I will set up one shepherd over them, and he shall feed them,
even my servant David (Ezek. 34.23) . . . and they shall know
that I the Lord their God am with them, and that they, the house
of Israel, are my people' (v. 30). It is impossible to question the
authenticity of Matt. 15.24: to a church which even before Paul's
time had accepted the Gentile mission (Acts 11.20 ff.), such a
'particularist' saying must have been repugnant in the highest
degree. It is hardly accidental that Matt. 15.24, as well as the
similar saying in Matt. 10.5 f., is absent from Mark and Luke.
Matthew's only reason for preserving the logion in spite of its
repellent implication was that it bore the stamp of the Lord's
authority.

R. Bultmann's argument against the authenticity of Matt.
15.24, namely that the use of ἀποσταλῆναι (or πεμφθῆναι) in John's
gospel 'is typical of the terminology of a later time',[1] will not
bear examination: in no passage of John's gospel is the passive
aorist of ἀποστέλλειν or πέμπειν used of Jesus' being sent. On the
contrary, throughout that gospel the active is regularly used of
the sending of Jesus (John 3.17: ἀπέστειλεν ὁ θεὸς τὸν υἱόν, etc.), and
hence indicates that the use of the passive as a circumlocution for
the divine name, as we find it in Matt. 15.24 (ἀπεστάλην), is characteristic of the early tradition. Neither can it be argued against
the authenticity of the saying that the use of the aorist ἀπεστάλην
appears 'to treat the historical advent of Jesus as something wholly
in the past';[2] for in Aramaic the perfect need not imply a past
event, but may just as well imply a perfect present (ἀπεστάλην is the
same as אֶשְׁתַּדָּרִית, i.e. 'God has sent me', 'my God-given commission relates to').

If it be granted then that purely linguistic considerations furnish
no argument against the authenticity of Matt. 15.24, but rather, as
we have seen, provide evidence for the existence of an underlying
Semitic text, the only question which remains is whether the
saying can have arisen 'out of the disputes in the Palestinian

[1] R. Bultmann, *History of the Synoptic Tradition*, ET Oxford 1963, pp.
155 f. [2] Ibid.

community concerning the Gentile mission'.[1] This view involves
many serious difficulties. In the first place the principle must be
laid down that, while it is an assured result of synoptic criticism
that already at an early date the church had reinterpreted many
sayings of Jesus, nevertheless the further assumption that the
earliest Aramaic-speaking community had already invented sayings of the Lord is unwarranted. But it is especially necessary to observe that if the rejection of the Gentile mission in Matt.
10.5 f. and 15.24 has been put into the mouth of Jesus by the
primitive community, then the stories in Mark 7.24 ff. and parallels, and Matt. 8.5 ff. and parallels, must be ascribed to the same
source, since they describe a similar rejection. But these two stories
have an entirely different point, for they both end by showing
Jesus as yielding to entreaty and healing the Gentile. If, nevertheless, we ascribe Matt. 15.24 and the two above-mentioned stories
to the invention of the primitive church, we shall find ourselves
involved in some very complicated theories: Matt. 15.24 must be
ascribed to the invention of a circle of the primitive Palestinian
church which was hostile to the Gentile mission, while Mark
7.24 ff., and Matt. 8.5 ff. will have emanated from a circle of the
primitive church which was favourable to the Gentile mission and
wished to refute the views of the opposing circle, and all this must
have already taken place before the passages in question were
translated into Greek. Nothing could be more utterly improbable.

But if Jesus had refused to engage in activities extending beyond the borders of Israel, the question at once arises of how we
are to reconcile this fundamental limitation of Jesus' mission with
the gospel stories which depict him as succouring the Gentiles.
The question is the more insistent as these stories recount acts of
healing. When Jesus heals, his act has eschatological significance,
and is always the sign and pledge of the breaking in of the Messianic age, an anticipatory participation in its blessings.

There are two synoptic stories which explicitly record en-
counters of Jesus with Gentiles, and both are healings at a distance: they are Matt. 8.5–13 (parallel in Luke 7.1–10, cf. John

[1] R. Bultmann, *History of the Synoptic Tradition*, ET Oxford 1963, p. 155
(slightly altered).

4.46–53) and Mark 7.24–30 (parallel in Matt. 15.21–28); a third may possibly be added, namely the story of the Gadarene demoniac, Mark 5.1–20 (parallels in Matt. 8.21–40 and Luke 8.26–39).[1]

The first thing which stands out in the story of the Syrophoenician woman is that Jesus refuses her request, and that extremely harshly: just as no one would think of feeding the dogs with the children's food, so Jesus could not entertain the proposal to give Israel's food to Gentiles (Mark 7.27); nor should it be forgotten that even today in the East the term 'dog' is the supreme insult, and even if we allow for the fact that Jesus used vivid imagery to make his refusal clear, the impression still remains that nowhere else did Jesus address a Gentile in such harsh terms.[2] Jesus cannot and ought not to help the woman since he has been sent to Israel and not to Gentiles. Certainly the story has a different ending from that which its beginning would lead us to expect.

---

[1] The scene of the story is in Decapolis (Mark 5.1, 20), inhabited by a mixed population; the herd of swine indicates a Gentile environment (5.11 and parallels). On the other hand, the story of the healing of the deaf-mute in Decapolis (Mark 7.31–37) hardly comes into question here. Indeed Matthew (although he does not relate the story itself, but gives instead a summary which describes the healing of all kinds of sick persons on a mountain by the Lake of Gennesaret, 15.29–31) seems to have understood it as the story of the healing of a Gentile, as the concluding words of the summary, καὶ ἐδόξασαν τὸν θεὸν Ἰσραήλ (15.31), would suggest. Mark, too, in framing his story, may have thought of the deaf-mute as a Gentile (see below p. 33). But the story itself does not point in this direction. On the contrary, it is most improbable that it depicted the deaf-mute as a Gentile, since the concluding exclamation of praise extols the miracle (v. 37), not the display of mercy to a Gentile.

[2] The text shows two mitigations of the original harshness of the saying: (a) the phrase in Mark 7.27a ἄφες πρῶτον χορτασθῆναι τὰ τέκνα has no counterpart in the parallel in Matt. 15.26. Through the use of the word πρῶτον implying an eschatological ὕστερον the exclusive privilege of Israel (Matt. 15.24) becomes in Mark a passing temporary right. But the suggestion of a period of delay, after the expiry of which mercy might be extended to the Gentiles, would be no comfort to the woman in her present anxiety about her daughter. Hence the πρῶτον is a mitigation which Mark found already in his source. The insertion of πρῶτον precludes the suggestion that Jesus was definitely opposed to the Gentile mission. (Cf. H. Stoevesandt, *Jesus und die Heidenmission*, p. 15.) (b) Mark 7.27 and Matthew 15.26 both have the diminutive κυνάριον. However, quite apart from the fact that it is uncertain whether in contemporary Greek the diminutive had any mitigating force, it cannot be pressed, since Semitic has no corresponding form. We must assume that Jesus used the word כַּלְבָּא (dog), and he is not likely to have used גּוּרָא ('cub', 'puppy').

The woman recognizes Jesus as the giver of the Bread of Life (7.28),[1] and this confession of faith overcomes his reluctance (7.29). But Jesus does not grant her request until she has recognized the divinely ordained division between God's people and the Gentiles[2].

We meet with what is essentially the same situation in the story of the centurion. Jesus' answer to the request of the Gentile should be read as a question, as is shown by a comparison with John 4.48: ἐγὼ ἐλθὼν θεραπεύσω αὐτόν; (Matt. 8.7). Again Jesus brusquely refuses,[3] and again the Gentile's answer is a confession of faith. The Syriac versions suggest that in the original Aramaic the centurion's answer may have read: 'You need only give the order and my servant will be healed, for I too have authority over the soldiers under my command' (Matt. 8.9); that is to say, 'You are the Lord, all power is yours, you can command the spirits'.[4] Once again Jesus yields to the suppliant's faith. Another case of a refusal occurs in the story of the Gadarene, although it is doubtful whether this quite belongs to the same type of story: in it Jesus refuses the request of the healed man to be allowed to follow him (Mark 5.19).[5] Clearly these stories must be regarded as excep-

---

[1] J. Jeremias, *The Parables of Jesus*[2], p. 118 n. 14.

[2] A. Schlatter, *Der Evangelist Matthäus*, Stuttgart 1929, p. 489.

[3] In order to avoid this harsh refusal, Luke has completely recast the introduction to the story (7.2–6a, 7a).

[4] The existing Greek text (καὶ γὰρ ἐγὼ ἄνθρωπός εἰμι ὑπὸ ἐξουσίαν [+τασσόμενος Luke], ἔχων ὑπ' ἐμαυτὸν στρατιώτας κτλ. Matt. 8.9; Luke 7.8) makes the centurion utter two strangely conflicting statements: first, that he is a man under authority, and therefore knows how to obey; then, that he has soldiers under him, and therefore knows how to command. The Syriac versions show that the centurion's words only envisage his own possession of authority (syr^sin Matt. 8.9 'for I also am a man דאית לי שולטנא *having authority*, and soldiers are under my hand'; syr^pal Matt. 8.9 'for I also am a man ואית תחות שולטנותי רומין and have those who are subject to *my authority*'; Eus. syr. *Theoph.* 4.2: 'for I also am a man דבשולטנא =ἐν ἐξουσίᾳ ='having authority'; cf. A. Merx, *Das Evangelium Matthäus*, Berlin 1902, pp. 133 f.). In Aramaic the text would have run בְּשׁוּלְטָנָא? =ἐν ἐξουσίᾳ (cf. Luke 4.36)='having authority'; the translator understood the words to mean 'under authority', i.e. 'having superiors over me', and rendered them by ὑπ' ἐξουσίαν.

[5] That Jesus charged the man whom he had healed to announce to his own people what God had done for him, does not alter the fact that Jesus did not

tions.[1] When, in addition, it is recognized that in all three cases the initiative is not taken by Jesus, it becomes abundantly clear that these stories afford no ground for assuming that Jesus extended his mission to the Gentiles, but, on the contrary, that they confirm the fact that he limited his activity to Israel.[2] This is further attested by Luke 13.16; 19.9, where Jesus bases and justifies his activity of succour and healing on the fact that he is extending it towards the seed of Abraham.

But the question still remains whether this limitation to Israel holds good for the whole of Jesus' ministry, or only for the first half. Not long after the feeding of the multitude, that is, after the passover of A.D. 29, a great division occurs in the external course of Jesus' life. Three factors contributed to bring this about: 1. Jesus' rejection became increasingly marked, and reached a definite break with the leaders of the people; 2. as a result, Jesus left Galilee and went into the district of Tyre (Mark 7.24, 31);[3]

---

grant his request to be allowed to become one of his followers. A comment on the strange passage in Mark 5.12–13 (the entry of the demons into the 2,000 swine) may be added here. It becomes clear that these verses are an expansion when we observe that in the preceding verses (vv. 2, 7–10a) and in the verse following (15), the demon is spoken of in the singular, and the plural only occurs in vv. 10b, 12–13. The insertion has arisen by reason of the ambiguity of the loan-word לִגְיוֹנָא? (v. 9), which in Aramaic may mean (1) 'soldier', and (2) 'legion'. In the reply of the demoniac in v. 9 the word is used in the first of these two meanings: 'My name is "Soldier", since we (the demons) are a great host (and resemble one another as soldiers do).' Owing to the fact that the translator rendered the word לִגְיוֹנָא? by the Greek λεγιών, the mistaken idea arose that the demoniac was possessed by a whole regiment of demons. The normal strength of a legion was 6,000 men, and the reduced number of 2,000 (v. 13) which has perplexed the commentators may possibly be explained on the supposition that whoever was responsible for the insertion had in mind the military unit of the τέλος ('legion', 'battalion'; in the capture of Jerusalem in 37 B.C., for instance, eleven τέλη of infantry were engaged, Jos. *Bell.* I, 346; *Ant.* XVI, 469): the strength of the τέλος was 2,048 men. Thus the original continuation of v. 11 was v. 14, and the herd of swine was only mentioned because the swineherds witnessed the expulsion of the demon (v. 14).

[1] Recently: T. W. Manson, *Jesus and the Non-Jews*, p. 18.

[2] Only by the Fourth Gospel is the fact mentioned that on one occasion Jesus had preached for a time (John 4.40: two days) to the Samaritans (4.4–42).

[3] In some important MSS the words καὶ Σιδῶνος are absent from Mark 7.24; in 7.31 we have the topographical indication: 'Then he returned from

(it is to be observed that both the synoptic accounts of the feeding of the multitude agree in giving the order of events as follows: the feeding, the clash with the Pharisees, the withdrawal into Gentile territory, Mark 7.24; 8.27.) 3. on this so-called northern journey follows the encounter with the Syrophoenician woman (Mark 7.24–30). The question thus arises whether, after the passover of A.D. 29, Jesus moved over to acceptance of the Gentile mission. We may ask whether such a reconstruction of the preceding events as the following is possible: Jesus is compelled[1] to withdraw into the region of the Phoenician coastal cities; it is not his intention to pursue his missionary activities in the north, but, on the contrary, he wishes to remain in concealment (Mark 7.24); but the faith of the Gentile woman shows him what is now God's will for him. In that case, Jesus' sharp refusal of the Syrophoenician woman's request would represent a last revulsion in his mind from such a revolutionary change in his outlook as the acceptance of the Gentile mission would represent, and we should have to divide the ministry of Jesus into two periods: up to the passover of A.D. 29 the proclamation to Israel, in his last year the Gentile mission.

Nevertheless, while this solution is possible on psychological

---

the region of Tyre, and went through Sidon (about 22 miles north of Tyre!) to the Sea of Galilee, right into the region of the Decapolis,' a very strange route. Since in the second account of the feeding of the multitude, in the parallel passage (cf. Mark 7.32 with 8.22), we are told that Jesus came εἰς Βηθσαϊδάν, the question arises whether the mention of Sidon in Mark 7.31 may not have arisen through a mishearing: 'I suggest that בצידן here should not have been rendered by διὰ Σιδῶνος, but by εἰς Βησσαιδαν: from Tyre he came to Bethsaida by the Sea of Galilee', is the brilliant conjecture of J. Wellhausen, *Das Evangelium Marci*,[2] Berlin 1909, p. 58 on 7.31. It is also possible that the mention of Sidon in Mark 7.24 v.l., 31 may be explained by the fact that 'Tyre and Sidon' had passed into general use as a formula for the pair of cities (Jer. 25.22; 27.3; 47.4; I Mac. 5.15; Judith 2.28; Matt. 11.21 f.; 15.21; Mark 3.8; Luke 6.17; 10.13 f.; extra-biblical examples are given in W. F. Arndt and F. W. Gingrich, *A Greek-English Lexicon of the New Testament*, Cambridge and Chicago 1957, p. 757. In view of these considerations, it must at least remain highly doubtful whether Jesus also entered the territory of Sidon (cf. also the questions raised by A. Alt in *Ztschr. d. Dtsch. Pal.-Vereins* 68, 1951, p. 71).

[1] Matt. 15.21: ἀνεχώρησεν always indicates the avoidance of danger by Jesus.

grounds, it is untenable, first on literary-critical grounds, and secondly on topographical grounds.

1. In two passages in Mark we have an account of the activity of Jesus among Gentiles. In 3.7 f. the evangelist describes a mighty gathering of people to Jesus. Not only do people flock to hear him from Galilee, Judaea, and Jerusalem, but 'a great multitude' comes also from Idumaea, Transjordan, and the region of the coastal cities of Tyre and Sidon. But it is clear that this enumeration does not rest on any concrete tradition, since it represents the introduction to a summary by the evangelist which includes 3.7–12, and which, on closer examination, is found to be a mosaic whose separate components are drawn from the various isolated traditions which were available to Mark; in particular the coupled cities 'Tyre and Sidon' are taken from 7.31.[1] A similar judgement must be arrived at with regard to the so-called 'northern journey' in Mark 7.24–8.26. The topographical details in 7.24, 31; 8.4, 13, 22, 27 might suggest that Mark intended this section to be a description of an extended activity among the Gentiles on the part of Jesus;[2] but an analysis of the section leads to the result that the only concrete material which the evangelist possessed for this supposed Gentile activity on the part of Jesus consisted of the story of the Syrophoenician woman.[3]

Luke, too, whose intense missionary interest is already indicated by the fact that he has added the Acts of the Apostles to his gospel, betrays a strong inclination to ascribe a missionary activity among the Gentiles to Jesus.[4] At the outset the child Jesus is designated by Simeon as φῶς εἰς ἀποκάλυψιν ἐθνῶν (2.32); the advent of the Baptist heralds the imminent fulfilment of the prophecy: καὶ ὄψεται πᾶσα σὰρξ τὸ σωτήριον τοῦ θεοῦ (3.6 = Isa. 40.5); by tracing back the genealogy of Jesus to God (3.38) the evangelist

---

[1] Idumaea (only here in the gospels) seems to have been inserted without any adequate evidence merely to round off the geographical description.

[2] Only in 8.10–13 is Jesus represented as passing through the western region of Jordan.

[3] Recently: V. Taylor, *The Gospel according to St Mark*, London 1952, Additional note D: 'The Journey of Jesus to the Region of Tyre', pp. 632–6.

[4] E. Lohse, 'Missionarisches Handeln Jesu nach dem Evangelium des Lukas', in *TZ* 10, 1954, pp. 1–13.

prepares his readers for the realization that the subject of his gospel is to be the Saviour of mankind. The inhabitants of Nazareth are forthwith warned of the transference of the good news to the Gentiles (4.25 ff.); particularistic sayings (e.g. Matt. 10.5 f., 23; 15.24) and the story of the Syrophoenician woman (Mark 7.24–30) are omitted; as we saw on p. 24, already during Jesus' lifetime the disciples have been sent to the Gentiles (Luke 10.1, cf. 14.23); a Samaritan is healed by Jesus (17.16)—but of what we are eagerly expecting to find in addition to this, namely, some description of Jesus' own activity among the Gentiles, there is no trace, except for the story of the centurion (7.1–10, with significant omission of Jesus' initial hesitation) and for the mention of the multitude that came to Jesus from Tyre and Sidon in the summary taken from Mark which has already been mentioned (6.17, parallel Mark 3.8). Here we have one of the most convincing proofs of Luke's fidelity to his sources. Although he had every inducement to adduce the example of Jesus as the authentication of the Gentile mission, he adhered closely to his sources and resisted the temptation to create concrete examples, even if only in the form of a summary.

Of the three synoptists Matthew evinces the strongest inclination to ascribe to Jesus a missionary activity among the Gentiles. He introduces the ministry of Jesus by a quotation which explicitly mentions the Gentiles: Zebulon and Naphthali, towards the lake, Transjordan and Γαλιλαία τῶν ἐθνῶν, the people in darkness and the shadow of death, they all see a great light (Matt. 4.15 f. =Isa. 8.23–9.1). Similarly he expands the Marcan summary (Mark 3.7–10) by the addition: 'And the report of him went forth into all Syria, and they (the inhabitants of Syria?) brought unto him all that were sick . . . and he healed them' (Matt. 4.24). With intentional emphasis Matthew has introduced the cycle of miracle-stories by the two accounts of Jesus healing the leper (8.1–4), and a Gentile, the centurion's servant (8.5–13), as extreme examples. He gives a quotation which says that in Jesus the prediction of the Servant of Jahveh is fulfilled: κρίσιν τοῖς ἔθνεσιν ἀπαγγελεῖ . . . καὶ τῷ ὀνόματι αὐτοῦ ἔθνη ἐλπιοῦσιν (12.18, 21 = Isa.

42.1, 4). In the interpretation (composed by Matthew himself[1]) of the parable of the Tares, Matthew uses the word κόσμος in a universal sense (13.37 f., the Son of Man sows the seed in a world-wide field), and in the parable of the Seine-net (13.47), the fishes ἐκ παντὸς γένους, whose variety was originally intended merely to point the need for selection (13.48), may have been allegorized to refer to the peoples of the world. While in 15.29–31 he appears to represent Jesus as exercising an activity among the Gentiles on a grand scale (cf. p. 29 n. 1), in actuality the only evidence he offers is, significantly, a summary. If we leave out of account quotations, summaries, and allegorical interpretations of parables, we find that Matthew yields the same result as Mark and Luke: the only solid evidence which the evangelists possess for Jesus' activity among the Gentiles consists of the accounts of the two cases of healing at a distance (Matt. 8.5–13 and parallel; Mark 7.24–30 and parallel), alongside of which the story of the Gadarene demoniac may perhaps be placed. That is all.

2. This result of literary criticism is confirmed by topographical considerations. In a thorough-going topographical study entitled *Die Stätten des Wirkens Jesu in Galiläa,*[2] Albrecht Alt has proved that *we have no evidence that Jesus ever went beyond the boundaries of the Jewish population.* His ministry lay in the hill-country of Galilee, with its almost purely Israelite population, and on the northern coast of the Lake of Gennesaret; the Hellenistic cities of Galilee, Sepphoris, only four miles from Nazareth, and Tiberias, only three and a half miles from Magdala, were evidently deliberately avoided by him.[3] Occasionally he extended his activity to the east shore of the lake; but here, too, he found a mixed population, of whom the great majority, nevertheless, especially in the country, practised the Jewish religion, evidence of which is provided by, among other things, the ruins of a synagogue near the hot springs

---

[1]In Matt. 13.36–43 no less than 37 linguistic peculiarities of the evangelist occur (J. Jeremias, *The Parables of Jesus*[2], pp. 82–4).

[2]In *Ztschr. d. Dtsch. Pal.-Vereins* 68, 1951, pp. 51–72=*Kleine Schriften zur Geschichte des Volkes Israel* II, Munich 1953, pp. 436–55.

[3]Ibid. pp. 63, 67 f.

in the Jarmuk valley.[1] The first occasion on which Jesus seems to
have left Jewish territory and to have passed over into Gentile
territory was on his journey to the region (τὰ ὅρια) of Tyre (and
Sidon?, see above p. 31 n. 3), Mark 7.24, 31, and during his
wandering among the 'villages' of Caesarea Philippi, 8.27. However, at that time the territories of Tyre and Sidon extended far
east into the interior: that of Tyre stretched over the whole of the
northern district of upper Galilee as far as the basin of Lake
Huleh, while that of Sidon extended as far as the territory of
Damascus.[2] If Jesus wished to pass from Galilee to the region
of Caesarea Philippi, he would of necessity have to touch Tyrian
territory.[3] This region lying between Galilee and Caesarea Philippi
had once been part of the kingdom of Israel, and talmudic statements about the boundaries of those parts of Palestine with an
Israelite population[4] prove that in the time of Jesus it was still
mainly inhabited by the descendants of the northern Israelite
tribes.[5] 'It would have been to these outposts of Israelite population and Jewish religion that the mind of Jesus first turned when
he extended his activity so far to the north. Even here, just as
there (by the Lake of Gennesaret), we find no real, not to say
final, crossing of the boundary of the Jewish population; and the
actual goal of his path, always consciously envisaged by Jesus, lay
not in Galilee, but in Jerusalem.'[6]

The conclusion that the synoptic gospels offer no support for
the conjecture that Jesus, disappointed by the rejection of his own
people, at the last directed his ministry towards the Gentiles, is

---

[1] *Ztschr. d. Dtsch. Pal.-Vereins* 68, 1951, pp. 69 f. Examples of Jewish
settlement on the east shore of the Lake of Gennesaret are given by G.
Dalman, *Orte und Wege Jesu*[3], Gütersloh 1924, pp. 181–4.

[2] A. Alt, op. cit. pp. 70 f.; G. Dalman, op. cit. p. 213.

[3] A. Alt, op. cit. p. 71. Since Kedesh was at that time part of Tyrian terri-
tory, according to Josephus (*Bell.* II, 459; IV, 104), Wadi 'Oba, leading to
Lake Simhu, must be regarded as the northern boundary of Galilee (G.
Dalman, op. cit. p. 213).

[4] G. Dalman, op. cit. pp. 219 f.

[5] A. Alt, op. cit. p. 72.

[6] Ibid. Already in 1924 G. Dalman had emphasized the fact that, even in
his journeys outside the contemporary boundaries of the Jewish territory,
Jesus 'never crossed the boundaries of the land of Israel' (op. cit. p. 219, cf.
p. 220).

confirmed from three sources. Paul provides the first confirmation. In Rom. 15.7 ff. he enjoins Jewish and Gentile Christians to live in fellowship with one another (v. 7) since they are both objects of divine grace (vv. 8–12). With regard to Jewish Christians he points out that Christ was a διάκονος τῆς περιτομῆς in order to fulfil the promises to the fathers (v. 8). With regard to the Gentile Christians Paul cannot similarly appeal to the fact that Jesus had preached to Gentiles, valuable as such an argument would have been in this connexion, but is obliged to fall back upon Scripture as the ground for their salvation (vv. 9–12); Paul adheres to the tradition, which has nothing to tell him about any ministry of Jesus to the Gentiles.[1]

The gospel of John presents the same picture. The very fact that this gospel departs in so many details from the actual life of Jesus, adapting its account to the circumstances of its own time, that is, to the situation of the church in Asia Minor at the close of the first century A.D., renders its testimony of the greatest weight with regard to the problem before us. It would not be surprising if the Fourth gospel had read back its own missionary situation into the life of Jesus; but the opposite has happened. Not until the final days, after the entry into Jerusalem, do we find Jesus coming into contact with Gentiles (Ἕλληνες), John 12.20 ff.[2] This is represented as an wholly unusual event, so unprecedented that Jesus explains that the hour has come for him to be glorified (12.23). But he immediately adds that the corn of wheat must first die (and rise again) in order that it may bring forth much fruit (v. 24).[3] Not until he is lifted up from the earth will he draw all

---

[1]C. H. Dodd, *History and the Gospel*, London 1938, p. 131. Does Rom. 9.30–33 also bear witness to the fact that Paul only knew of Jesus' ministry in Israel? Cf. J. Munck, *Paul and the Salvation of Mankind* p. 273 n. 1: 'In 9.30–33 we hear only of Jesus' earthly life in Palestine, his rejection by the Jews, and his crucifixion.'

[2]John 4.46–53 can only be an exception if John regarded the βασιλικός (4.46, 49) not as a Jew (so Spitta, Bauer, Schlatter, Büchsel, Bultmann), but as a Gentile (so Strathmann).

[3]'But if it die, it bringeth forth much fruit': the form of the saying follows the oriental mode of expression which concentrates only on the initial stage (the death) and on the final stage (the fruit, i.e. the world redeemed), and needs to be completed by the indispensable intermediate event (the

men unto him (v. 32, cf. 11.51 f.). Not until he is glorified will he exercise the ἐξουσία πάσης σαρκός, the authority to give life to as many as the Father has given him (17.1 f.). It is not by accident that the saying in John 10.16 about the 'other sheep' comes after the announcement of his laying down his life (v. 15). Hence the Fourth gospel repeatedly emphasizes the fact the hour of the Gentiles (the μείτονα ἔργα of 14.12) can only come after the Cross.

Similarly, the principle that the hour of the Gentiles can only come after the Cross and the Resurrection underlies the missionary commission of Matt. 28.18–20. In my discussion of I Tim. 3.16, I have pointed out that the credal confession which that passage contains is couched in the form of a hymn of three distichs, after the style of a coronation hymn; the ancient coronation ritual, exemplified for us in the ancient Egyptian ritual, consisted of three actions: 1. The Elevation; 2. the Presentation or Proclamation; 3. the Enthronement of the new king. Similarly, we find in I Tim. 3.16 in three successive distichs: 1. the Justification by resurrection of him who has been manifested on earth; 2. the announcement to heaven and earth of his Exaltation; and 3. his assumption of the Kingdom on earth and in heaven.[1] This triple-action form of coronation hymn occurs in the New Testament not only in I Tim. 3.16, but also elsewhere, for example, in Phil. 2.9–11 (1. Elevation in v. 9a; 2. Proclamation of the Name above every name in v. 9b; 3. homage to the Enthroned one by gesture and confession v. 10 f.);[2] also in Heb. 1.5–14 (1. Elevation as Son of God v.5 f.; 2. Proclamation of his eternal Kingship

---

resurrection); on this mode of expression cf. J. Jeremias, *The Parables of Jesus*[2], p. 148 n. 75; there a reference is made to M. Rissi, *Zeit und Geschichte in der Offenbarung des Johannes*, Zürich 1952, p. 44, who gives Rev. 12.5 as a further example, where the birth and the assumption occur in immediate succession, without the neccesary intermediate stage of the earthly life.

[1] *Die Briefe des Timotheus und Titus* (= NTD9), Göttingen 1934 (8th ed. 1963), ad loc.
[2] Cf. E. Käsemann, 'Kritische Analyse von Phil. 2, 5–11', in *Exegetische Versuche und Besinnungen I*, Göttingen 1960, pp. 51–95.

vv. 7–12; 3. Enthronement v. 13 f.).[1] We are indebted to Otto Michel for the significant recognition that in Matt. 28.18–20 also we have a triple-action coronation text: 1. in v. 18 we have the Assumption of all power by the Risen One; 2. in vv. 19–20a there follows the injunction to proclaim his authority among all nations; 3. v. 20b closes with the word of power καὶ ἰδοὺ ἐγὼ μεθ' ὑμῶν εἰμι πάσας τὰς ἡμέρας[2] ἕως τῆς συντελείας τοῦ αἰῶνος, which is to be understood in the light of Luke 10.19; (Ps.–) Mark 16.17 f.: the Son of Man displays his royal power in his guardianship of his messengers.[3] Hence the implication of Matt. 28.18–20 is that with the death and resurrection of Jesus the eschatological hour has arrived.[4] God no longer limits his saving grace to Israel, but turns in mercy to the whole Gentile world. Henceforth the eschatological people of God are to announce to all nations that they too belong to the kingdom of the Son of Man. In such wise does the closing passage of the Matthaean gospel indirectly establish the fact that the earthly ministry of Jesus had not yet embraced the Gentiles.

We have entitled this first section *Three Important Negative Conclusions,* and we now find ourselves confronted by a finding whose severity may not be minimized by apologetic arts. Was the ministry of Jesus wholly limited to Judaism?

---

[1]O. Michel, *Der Brief an die Hebräer*, Göttingen 1936, p. 26 (6th ed. 1966, pp. 116 f.); E. Käsemann, *Das wandernde Gottesvolk*, Göttingen 1938, pp. 59 ff.

[2]A Semitism='for ever' (Semitic has no other means of expressing time in the durative sense).

[3]O. Michel, 'Der Abschluss des Matthäusevangeliums', in *Ev. Th.* 10, 1950–51, pp. 16–26. In n. 86 Michel correctly remarks that the words 'I am with you' in the Bible are often a circumlocution for the divine protection (Gen. 28.15; Judg. 6.12; Acts 18.10 *et al.*).

[4]C. H. Dodd, *New Testament Studies*, Manchester 1953, p. 56, makes the same point when, in agreement with R. H. Lightfoot, he describes Matt. 28.16–20 as 'a kind of proleptic παρουσία'.

II

THREE IMPORTANT POSITIVE CONCLUSIONS

HITHERTO we have accepted the way in which the scholarship of the past has stated the problem, and have asked what was the attitude of Jesus towards the Gentile mission. But this way of stating the problem is not only insufficient but false, since it ignores the eschatological character of the message of Jesus. Hence progress will only be possible if we avoid this erroneous approach and attempt to answer the broader question of what Jesus actually says about the nations.[1] So formulated, the question yields a very different picture in reply.

Again we must begin with Jesus' environment. The attitude of late Judaism towards non-Jews was uncompromisingly severe.[2] In addition to their abhorrence of idolatry, their attitude was largely determined by the oppression which they had undergone at the hands of foreign nations, and by their fear of the increasing prevalence of mixed marriages. Thus it is easy to understand why to them the Gentiles were godless, rejected by God, as worthless in his eyes as chaff and refuse;[3] they were steeped in vice; they were given over to every form of uncleanness, violence, and wickedness.[4] This estimate of the Gentiles was reflected in the popular eschatology. The Messiah of popular expectation would deliver the Jewish people from foreign domination and establish a glorious kingdom. There were differing views concerning the final fate of the Gentiles. An early universalistic tendency, in

[1]B. Sundkler, 'Jésus et les païens' (with reference to the remarks of A. Schweitzer, *The Mysticism of Paul the Apostle*, pp. 176–80), has performed the great service of emphasizing the correct statement of the problem. In agreement with him is H. Stoevesandt, *Jesus und die Heidenmission*.

[2]Heb. *goyim,* Aram. *'am^emayya,* Gr. ἔθνη.

[3]Billerbeck III, pp. 139 ff.; IV, pp. 353 ff.

[4]Ibid. III, pp. 64, 140 ff.; IV, pp. 354 ff.

agreement with Old Testament prophecy, assigned a full participation in the future glory of Israel to the Gentiles, either in their
totality, or at least to those nations which had not been guilty of
the oppression of Israel.[1] In some quarters, however, this participation was severely limited, and it was held, in agreement with
some late passages of the Old Testament, such as Isa. 61.5 f., that
the Gentiles would become bondslaves of Israel, or that only on
payment of tribute would they be allowed to enter the land of
Israel.[2] On the other hand the dominant popular expectation
eagerly awaited the day of the divine vengeance, especially on
Rome,[3] and the final destruction of the Gentiles. 'No Gentile will
have a part in the world to come', was the teaching of that con-
sistent upholder of the ancient tradition, R. Eliezer ben Hyrcanus
(*circa* A.D. 90).[4] Hell is the destiny of the Gentiles.[5] 'There is no
ransom for the Gentiles . . . since the Holy One has given the
nations of the world as Israel's substitute, as an atonement for
their life (see Isa. 43.3).'[6] It is not hard to understand how the
hatred of an oppressed people should find expression in the
popular eschatological expectation. If we contrast with this popular expectation what Jesus says about the Gentiles, we shall find
that it yields a threefold result.

A. JESUS REMOVES THE IDEA OF VENGEANCE FROM THE
   ESCHATOLOGICAL EXPECTATION

Jesus plainly declared the distinction between Israel and the
nations of the world in the divine plan of redemption. Israel is the
people of the covenant: she is the vineyard of God (Mark 12.1 ff.
and parallels), and his flock (Matt. 10.6; 15.24); as the seed of
Abraham she is the object of his saving love (Luke 13.16; 19.9),
and the recipient of the promise of the Kingdom (Matt. 8.12).
The Gentiles, on the other hand, are far from God, they are concerned only with their material needs (Matt. 6.32 parallel Luke

[1]Billerbeck III, pp. 144, 150–2.
[2]Ibid. III, pp. 144, 148 ff.
[3]Ibid. III, pp. 144 ff.
[4]Tos. Sanh. 13.2.
[5]Billerbeck III, pp. 63, 145, 154 f.; IV, pp. 1066 f.
[6]Mekh. Ex. 21.30.

12.30); their benevolence extends only to their compatriots (Matt. 5.47); their rulers are despots (Mark 10.42); their prayer is a vain repetition (Matt. 6.7); even when they are God's instruments (Luke 21.24; Mark 10.33), they use their power destructively. In these contrasts between Israel and the nations, which find their sharpest expression in Mark 7.27 and parallels, Jesus is following the Scriptures.

But Jesus wholly rejects any nationalistic sentiment of hate. This appears most clearly in the Samaritan stories of the gospels. The relations between the Jews and the Samaritans had undergone considerable changes in the pre-New Testament period. When they seceded from the Jewish community in the fourth century B.C.,[1] the Samaritans erected a temple on the summit of Mount Gerizim near Shechem, whither they brought the offerings prescribed in the Pentateuch, their sacred book. When, in December of 128 B.C.,[2] John Hyrcanus destroyed this temple, the enmity between Jews and Samaritans grew into a burning hatred.[3] Herod the Great seems to have pursued a policy of appeasement, which may be deduced from the two circumstances that he had married a Samaritan wife,[4] and that in his time Samaritans evidently had the privilege of entry into the inner court of the Temple.[5] But his policy was not destined to succeed. About A.D. 8 at night during the passover, the Samaritans scattered human bones in the Temple,[6] and this shocking defilement of the sanctuary by contact with dead bodies, which was evidently an act of revenge, caused the ancient hatred to break out with renewed bitterness. Now the Jews forbade marriage and trade with the Samaritans whom they stigmatized as a mixed race, and in matters of religious

---

[1] It is hardly possible to give a more precise date for this event, since the Samaritan sources (see J. Jeremias, 'Die Passahfeier der Samaritaner', *ZATW* Beih. 59, Giessen 1932, p. 57 n. 7) and Josephus (*Ant.* XI, 324; cf. XIII, 256) disagree.

[2] Jos. *Ant.* XIII, 254–6: after the death of Antiochus VII (129 B.C.) and the subsequent siege of Madaba, which lasted six months; Meg. Ta'an. (ed. G. Dalman, *Aramäische Dialektproben*,[2] Leipzig 1927, pp. 2, 11): on 21 Chislev (= Nov./Dec.).

[3] The Jewish reflection of its bitterness may be seen in Test. Levi 7.

[4] Her name was Malthace: Jos. *Bell.* I, 562; *Ant.* XVII, 20.

[5] Jos. *Ant.* XVIII, 30.   [6] Ibid. XVIII, 29 f.

observance placed them on a level with Gentiles. This was the situation in the time of Jesus as the gospels bear witness:[1] the Samaritan in Luke 17.18 is called ἀλλογενής, i.e. a Gentile,[2] and Σαμαρίτης is a term of reproach (John 8.48) by which the Jews express the depth of their contempt for the bastard race.[3] The Samaritans retort in kind: Luke 9.51 ff.; John 4.9. Against such a background of implacable hatred the significance of Jesus' actions becomes clear, as he extends to the Samaritan leper the same healing power as to his Jewish fellow-sufferers (Luke 17.11–19), or when he holds up to his compatriots a Samaritan as a shaming example of neighbourly love conquering national enmity (Luke 10.25–37) and of thankfulness towards God (17.18); or again, when he sharply condemns the anger against the inhospitable Samaritans apparently justly displayed by his disciples (9.55). A similar attitude is shown by Jesus towards the Romans. When the news is brought to him, a Galilean, of the dreadful massacre perpetrated by the legionaries upon his fellow-Galileans, to the astonishment of his hearers no trace of hate appears in his reply, but only a summons to Israel to repent (13.1–5).

But of still deeper import is the fact that Jesus *detaches the nationalistic idea of revenge from the hope of redemption.*

We find this already implied in the temptation-stories; for in all three versions of the narrative[4] the rejection of the nationalistic

[1]In the more recent literature (see e.g. E. Schürer, op. cit. II⁴, pp. 22 f., and also in Billerbeck I, pp. 538 ff.) this state of affairs is obscured by a failure to recognize the fact that the early Mishnaic prescriptions relating to the Samaritans come for the most part from the 2nd century A.D., a period during which the relations between the Jews and the Samaritans had temporarily improved. The final breach came about in the 3rd century. Cf. J. Jeremias, *Jerusalem zur Zeit Jesu* IIB, ch. 10: Die Samaritaner, pp. 224–31 = ²1962, pp. 387–394; *TWNT* VII, pp. 88–94.

[2]Cf. Concordance to the LXX, s.v. ἀλλογενής.

[3]Luke 10.37: The scribe uses a circumlocution because he is unwilling to use the term 'Samaritan'.

[4]Mark 1.12 f. shows that the account of the temptation in the wilderness existed as an independent unit of tradition; the same conclusion may be drawn from the Gospel of the Hebrews (ed. E. Klostermann, *Kleine Texte* 8³, Berlin 1929, p. 7 no.5) with regard to the temptation on the mountain (E. Lohmeyer, in *ZST* 14, 1937, pp. 619–50). It may be conjectured that in Matt. 4.1–11; Luke 4.1–13 three versions of the temptation-story have been combined.

Messianic expectation appears as the central issue (cf. also John 6.15).[1] Jesus is not the Messiah of Israel's expectation; it is not his business to set up the kingdom of Israel, but the Kingdom of God; he has not come to deliver his people from the yoke of Rome, but from Satan's bondage.

But we have even more significant examples. Special mention must be made of Luke 4.16 ff. The Lucan account of the rejection of Jesus in Nazareth is particularly noteworthy for the sudden and completely motiveless change of attitude on the part of his hearers. At first Jesus' audience is spell-bound by the 'gracious words' which fall from his lips; then follow immediately bitterest criticism and rejection, finally reaching a murderous pitch. The contradiction becomes apparent in v. 22; the beginning and the end of the verse are at variance with one another; the first two clauses would seem to express entranced wonder, the third, on the other hand, expresses sudden disbelief and criticism. But the first clause is ambiguous: καὶ πάντες ἐμαρτύρουν αὐτῷ (אַסְהֲדִין עֲלוֹהִי). The dative after μαρτυρεῖν can be either the dative of advantage (to bear witness *on behalf of* some one), or the dative of disadvantage (to bear witness *against* some one).[2] This ambiguity arises from the nature of Jewish law which knows nothing of counsel for prosecution or defence, but only witnesses, who either bring charges against the defendant as hostile witnesses, or bring evidence in his favour. Hence it is by no means certain whether the first clause in Luke 4.22 means 'they all bore witness *for* him', or has the possible meaning 'they all bore witness *against* him'. The deciding factor is the interpretation which we place upon the second clause: καὶ ἐθαύμαζον ἐπὶ τοῖς λόγοις τῆς χάριτος τοῖς ἐκπορευομένοις ἐκ τοῦ στόματος αὐτοῦ. First of all, it must be pointed out that θαυμάζειν can express both admiring astonishment, and

---

[1] J. Jeremias, *The Parables of Jesus*[2], p. 123.

[2] Blass-Debrunner § 188.1; W. F. Arndt–F. W. Gingrich, *Lexicon of the N.T*, p. 493. For a similar ambiguity of the Heb. הֵעִיד with suff. cf. Gesenius-Buhl, *Handwörterbuch über das A.T.*,[15] Leipzig 1910, p. 563a. Similarly in Aramaic אַסְהֵד עַל has the meaning 'to bear witness *for* anyone' (Targ. Job 16.19; 29.11; b. Ber. 30b), and also 'to bear witness *against* anyone' (Targ. Job 16.8).

opposition to what is strange,[1] and that οἱ λόγοι τῆς χάριτος in this Semitic Greek[2] does not mean 'words full of charm', 'gracious words', but 'words of (God's) mercy':[3] 'they were astonished that he spoke of the mercy of God'. Why should the people of Nazareth be astonished that Jesus spoke of God's mercy? Did they expect something else? The answer to our question will appear if we observe that the passage which Jesus took as the text of his address breaks off strangely in the middle of a sentence.[4] The words, 'to proclaim the acceptable year of the Lord' (Luke 4.19 =Isa. 61.2), are immediately followed in the Old Testament text by the concluding words, 'and a day of vengeance of our God' (Isa. 61.2). Jesus leaves out the day of vengeance! Hence they are —not astonished, but enraged. 'They protested with one voice (πάντες ἐμαρτύρουν αὐτῷ) and were furious (καὶ ἐθαύμαζον), because he (only) spoke about (God's year of) mercy (and omitted the words about the Messianic vengeance)'. Here the third clause comes in aptly: 'and said, Is not this the son of Joseph?'[5] He has not studied, he is not ordained, how dare he presume to announce the coming of the Messianic age, and by what right does he take upon himself to mutilate Holy Writ? All this implies that Luke 4.22 exhibits no break in the attitude of his audience towards Jesus. On the contrary it records that from the outset unanimous rage was their response to the message of Jesus. The good news was their stumbling block, principally because Jesus had removed vengeance on the Gentiles from the picture of the future.

The proof that nothing, withal, has been inserted into the text, may be found in the fact that in the saying of Jesus in Matt. 11.5 f., parallel in Luke 7.22 f., we meet with a similar situation. Why should anyone be offended because the blind receive their sight,

---

[1] G. Bertram, *TWNT* III, pp. 27–42.

[2] The examples collected by B. Violet, 'Zum rechten Verständnis der Nazareth-Perikope', in *ZNTW* 37, 1938, pp. 251–71, might be considerably increased.

[3] Ibid. pp. 264–7.

[4] We are indebted to K. Bornhäuser, *Das Wirken des Christus*[2], Gütersloh 1924, p. 59, for having drawn attention to this fact.

[5] The absence of the article before υἱός in Luke 4.22, points to an underlying construct state.

the lame walk, the dead are raised? An obvious cause of offence might be that it was the poor to whom the gospel was preached. But the cause of offence lies deeper. Jesus had quoted in a free rendering the prophetic promise in Isa. 35.5 f. (blind, deaf, lame), and had added (perhaps influenced by Isa. 29.18 f., deaf, blind, poor, and meek) Isa. 61.1: 'to the poor the gospel is preached'. In all three passages from Isaiah reference is made to the eschatological day of vengeance (Isa. 35.4: 'Your God will come with vengeance';[1] 29.20: 'The terrible one is brought to nought'; 61.2: 'And a day of vengeance of our God'). It is surely not accidental that the note of vengeance is absent from Jesus' saying. Happy is the man who is not offended because the Messianic age wears a different aspect from that which he had expected, and that, instead of God's vengeance, it promises God's tender mercy for the poor.

Jesus certainly spoke about divine retribution (ἐκδίκησις) in Luke 18.7: 'And shall not God avenge his elect (οὐ μὴ ποιήσῃ τὴν ἐκδίκησιν τῶν ἐκλεκτῶν αὐτοῦ) which cry to him day and night, even if he puts their patience to the test?'[2] But here there is clearly no question of political revenge in the form of the eschatological destruction of the Gentiles, but of punishment for the persecutors of Jesus' disciples and the resulting vindication of God's elect before the world.

B. JESUS PROMISES THE GENTILES A SHARE IN SALVATION

The negative observation that Jesus purged the eschatological expectation of the element of political revenge is, so to speak, only the reverse side of what he had to say about the final fate of the Gentiles. Of greater significance is the validation of the fact that he assured to Gentiles too a share in salvation.

[1] For the reference to Isa. 35.4 I am indebted to G. Bornkamm.
[2] On the translation of the Aramaizing sentence-structure see J. Jeremias, *The Parables of Jesus*[2], pp. 154 f., in agreement with H. Riesenfeld, 'Zu μακροθυμεῖν (Lk. 18, 7)', in *Neutestamentliche Aufsätze. Festschrift für Prof. J. Schmid*, Regensburg 1963, pp. 214-7. On the translation of ἐκδίκησιν ποιεῖν ('to vindicate'), cf. G. Schrenk, *TWNT* II, p. 444.

Gentiles also will have a part in the resurrection. This was Jesus' declaration: not only the Ninevites and the Queen of Sheba,[1] but also the inhabitants of Tyre and Sidon,[2] and even those of Sodom[3] and Gomorrha.[4] This was not something that could be taken for granted. It was for instance a subject of current discussion whether the men of Sodom would rise again. We learn once more (see above p. 41) from R. Eliezer ben Hyrcanus (*circa* A.D. 90) what was the ancient teaching on the point: 'The people of Sodom will *not* rise again'.[5] Jesus, on the other hand, says, They will rise again as certainly as Israel's dead.[6] All nations without exception will stand before the throne of the Son of Man (Matt. 25.31 ff.). The universality of the expression 'all nations' is borne out by the sayings already quoted about the judgement of the Gentiles of ancient times, and is confirmed by the impressive late-Jewish picture of the last judgement in b.Aboda Zara 2a, where the Romans, the Persians, the rest of the nations, and finally those Gentiles who have borne witness for Israel, appear successively before the judgement seat of God.[7] Then will the full severity of God's judgement be meted out to the Gentiles, but at the same time many of them will hear from the lips of the Son of Man God's welcome sentence of absolution: 'Come, ye blessed of my Father, inherit the kingdom prepared for you from the foundation of the world'[8] (Matt. 25.34). Jesus' audience must indeed have been surprised and amazed to hear such words. These words include not only those Gentiles who received Jesus and believed on him,[9] but also those who repented at the prophet's message,[10] those who

[1] Matt. 12.41 f., parallel Luke 11.31 f.

[2] Matt. 11.22, parallel Luke 10.14.

[3] Matt. 10.15, parallel Luke 10.12; Matt. 11.24.

[4] Matt. 10.15. On the linguistic antiquity of the passages referred to in notes 1–4, see below pp. 50 f.

[5] Ab. R. Nathan 36 (Tos. Sanh. 13.8, the same from an anonymous source; M. Sanh. 10.3, R. Nehemiah [*circa* 150 A.D.] follows the teaching of R. Eliezer). Cf. W. Bacher, *Die Agada der Tannaiten* I², p. 135.

[6] Israel's dead: Mark 12.18–27 and parallels.

[7] Billerbeck IV, pp. 1203–6; cf. the whole excursus on pp. 1199–1212, to which should be added at the foot of p. 1202 a reference to Syr. Bar. 72.2–6.

[8] The passive ἡτοιμασμένην is a circumlocution for the divine activity.

[9] Matt. 8.10.

[10] Matt. 12.41, parallel Luke 11.32.

submitted themselves to the Wisdom of God,[1] and who showed kindness to the hidden and unrecognized Messiah whom they encountered in the guise of the poor and suffering.[2] Such would be numbered among the people of God at the last day, and would sit down with the patriarchs in the Kingdom of God.[3]

The definiteness with which Jesus assigns to the Gentiles a share in the Kingdom of God becomes clear when we consider the sayings in which Israel and the Gentiles are contrasted. The most far-reaching announcements about the Gentiles occur in the sternest warnings and summons to repentance addressed by Jesus to Israel.

It has already been pointed out that Jesus, in accordance with the Old Testament, clearly asserted the fundamental distinction between Israel and the nations of the world in regard to God's redemptive purpose (see above pp. 41 f.). It was Israel's privilege as the vessel of the promises (Matt. 8.12: οἱ υἱοὶ τῆς βασιλείας) to receive the first offer of salvation. Nevertheless, we are not told that Jesus shared the views of his compatriots about Israel's superiority.

According to the popular view in the time of Jesus, Israel's superiority over the Gentiles consisted in the fact that Israel, by virtue of its lineal descent from Abraham, enjoyed the benefits of the vicarious merits of the patriarchs, and the consequent assurance of final salvation. It was the current belief that no descendant of Abraham could be lost.[4]

[1] Matt. 12.42, parallel Luke 11.31.
[2] Matt. 25.31–46. The assertion, made in all seriousness, that, with the help of analogies drawn from such sources as the Egyptian Book of the Dead, the authenticity of Matt. 25. 31–46 can be disputed, is, I must confess, one of the most inconceivable suggestions which have appeared in recent N.T. literature. Everyone knows how, in the Book of the Dead or in Midrashic literature, the dead man complacently and self-righteously proclaims his deeds of charity, and how, in rabbinic descriptions of the Last Judgement (Billerbeck IV, pp. 1199 ff.), the theme is always the confusion and condemnation of the Gentiles and the salvation of Israel. One has only to compare all this with Matt. 25.31–46 to see how every trace of self-confidence or of the idea of merit is absent, and how the Son of Man identifies himself here with the humblest; and it becomes clear that the two conceptions are worlds apart (cf. J. Jeremias, *The Parables of Jesus*[2], pp. 206–9).
[3] Matt. 8.11, parallel Luke 13.29.
[4] Billerbeck I, pp. 116 ff., especially the top of p. 120. On the fundamental significance of pure descent for the whole social structure of Judaism in the

The Baptist had already vehemently attacked this perilous assurance of salvation (Matt. 3.9, parallel in Luke 3.8), and Jesus had followed him in this. Jesus' attack is to be found, not only in the gospel of John, in the great discourse in John 8.31–59, in which the Jews who boasted of being Abraham's children are plainly called children of the devil (8.44), but also in the first three gospels. Jesus denied the claim that descent from Abraham could save a man from hell (Luke 16.26), and never wearied of calling his people to repentance. The mere fact of belonging to Israel constituted no protection against the judgement of God (13.6–9).[1] *In the final judgement the distinction between Israel and the Gentiles would disappear.* Exactly the same justice would be meted out to Israel as to the Gentiles; indeed, under certain circumstances, her punishment would be more severe. The fate awaiting Israel if she persisted in her impenitent rejection of the good news was a terrible one. Rivers of blood would flow from the Roman sword (Luke 13.1–3), the people would be decimated by natural disasters (13.4 f.), destruction would befall Jerusalem, guilty of the blood of the prophets (as the capital she here represents the whole nation), the Temple would be razed to the ground (Matt. 23.37 f. and parallels; Mark 13.2 and parallels). But all these disasters would be only the prelude to the final judgement of God.

Jesus illustrated the terrible nature of the judgement which awaited his unrepentant contemporaries by a comparison with the fate which had befallen the ancient heathen cities. On the authority of Gen. 13–18, Sodom and Gomorrha were regarded as the scene of the vilest heathen practices ('the deeds of the men of Sodom were dark as evening and night'[2]), Tyre and Sidon,

---

time of Jesus cf. J. Jeremias, *Jerusalem zur Zeit Jesu* IIB, pp. 141 ff. = [2]1962, pp. 304 ff. The importance of attested descent lies in the fact that it is a condition of future salvation (pp. 172–4).

[1]Other instances of the comparison of Israel with the fig-tree are to be found in Joel 1.7; Hosea 9.10 (cf. Jer. 24.1–10); Mark 11.11–14 and parallels; Apoc. of Peter 2.

[2]Tanh. to Gen. 19.24 (ed. S. Buber, Wilna 1885, p. 49b. 4). For rabbinical material about the depravity of Sodom and Gomorrha see Billerbeck I, pp. 571 ff.

according to Ezek. 26–28, typified the heathen sin of *hubris* towards God, and the severity of their punishment would correspond to the heinousness of their sins. But far sterner, said Jesus, would be the judgement which threatened Chorazin, Bethsaida, and Capernaum (Matt. 11.20–24 and parallels, cf. 10.15).[1]

But the full severity of the judgement that threatened Israel if she persisted in her unrepentant state is not conveyed even by the unadorned statement of Jesus that it would be more terrible than the punishment that awaited Sodom and Gomorrha. How Jesus envisaged the ultimate horror of this judgement finds expression in three sayings agreeing in meaning, though differing widely in imagery. 'The men of Nineveh will rise up in the judgement (as accusers) against this generation,[2] and will provide the criterion for its judgement;[3] for they repented at the preaching of Jonah, and behold, what is greater than Jonah is here. The queen of the South will rise up in the judgement (as an accuser) against this generation,[4] and will provide the criterion for its judgement;[5] for she came from the end of the earth to hear the wisdom of Solomon, and behold, what is greater than Solomon is here' (Matt. 12.41 f., parallel Luke 11.32, 31). Gentiles, putting Israel to shame, will provide the measure of her guilt. They had shown by their behaviour that they would gladly have received the message. Thus the unconceivable thing will come to pass: the γενεά of

---

[1] An early Aramaic tradition. In addition to linguistic and stylistic (parallelism) features, the antiquity of the logion is also evident from the fact that only here is there a reference to the activity of Jesus in Chorazin.

[2] Ἀνίστασθαι (ἐγείρεσθαι) μετά τινος does not mean here 'to rise together with anyone', but, as a Semitism, it is the same as קוּם עִם 'to appear in court with some one', no doubt as a hostile witness, hence 'to appear against (עִם) anyone as an accuser' (Heb. Ps. 94.16; Aram. Targ. Isa. 54.17; j. Qid. III, 64a.20; in the last passage קוּם עַם has the strong meaning 'to bring an action against anyone', cf. G. Dalman, *The Words of Jesus*, Edinburgh 1902, p. 64.

[3] Κατακρίνειν τινά does not mean here that the Gentiles will exercise judicial functions ('pronounce sentence upon anyone'), but it is another Semitism implying hostile testimony, 'to bring a charge against anyone'. (It is the same as חָיַב, e.g. Dan. 1.10, cf. J. Wellhausen, *Das Evangelium Matthaei*, Berlin 1904, p. 65.) Here it means, 'to provide the criterion for judgement upon anyone'. Cf. Sir. 11.18 Heb.; Rom. 2.27 (κρινεῖ); Mekh. Ex. 12.1; b. Baba Mezia 3b.

[4] See above n. 2.

[5] See above n. 3.

Israel, having rejected Jesus, will be condemned, and will undergo the bitter experience of seeing Gentiles find mercy. The story of God's saving activity shows this to be no idle threat. More than once already God had proved that he was not tied to Israel. The second of the sayings referred to above, one based on an early Aramaic tradition, Luke 4.25–27,[1] tells how, in the days of Elijah, it was not the will of God to show his favour to any one of the many widows in Israel by sending the prophet to them, but only to the Gentile widow in Zarephath; and again, in the days of Elisha, not one of the many lepers in Israel was healed, but only Naaman the Syrian (Luke 4.25–27): so it may happen to Israel at the end; mercy will be extended to the Gentiles, and *Israel will be excluded*, at any rate the living generation of Israelites. The third saying is equally severe and equally devoid of hope for Israel: Matt. 8.11 f., parallel Luke 13.28 f. The full horror of the threat that in the final judgement Gentiles will take the place of the sons of the Kingdom can best be measured by the fact that no Jewish scholar and no Jewish apocalyptist had ever dared to utter such a thing, and only to the Baptist, in Matt. 3.9, is a similar saying attributed.

C. THE REDEMPTIVE ACTIVITY AND LORDSHIP OF JESUS INCLUDES THE GENTILES

The message of salvation offered to the Gentiles by Jesus remains incomprehensible unless we realize that it is based on Jesus' consciousness of authority. This will appear from four examples.

1. First we must consider the title Son of Man. The doubts which have been expressed as to whether Jesus used the title have now been widely silenced, since ὁ υἱὸς τοῦ ἀνθρώπου is a Semitism

---

[1] Ἐπ᾽ ἀληθείας v. 25 (=ἀμήν); ἐν ταῖς ἡμέραις v. 25 (ἡμέραι='time' in the sense of duration, see above p. 39 n. 2); here are three examples of the circumlocution for the divine name by the use of the passive, vv. 25, 26, 27; the three and a half years' drought in the time of Elijah, v. 25 (a Palestinian tradition, not found in the Biblical narrative, cf. G. Kittel, *Rabbinica*, Leipzig 1920, pp. 31 ff.); paratactic καί with adversative meaning in v. 26 beginning and v. 27b; οὐδεμία . . . . εἰ μή v. 26, οὐδεὶς . . . . εἰ μή v. 27 (= אֶלָּא . . . . לֹא).

which, on account of its ambiguity (as though it might be an indication of descent, while, in fact, *bar naša* means 'man') soon disappeared from Greek usage. Hence at least the statements about the parousia of the Son of Man are now recognized by many as authentic sayings of Jesus. Discussion today turns much more on the question of the authenticity of the passages in which the suffering of the Son of Man is referred to, and whether Jesus regarded himself as the Son of Man, or only as the forerunner and herald of the coming Son of Man. But if, with what I regard as an excessive and unwarranted scepticism, such a possibility be entertained, namely, that Jesus did not identify himself with the Son of Man, and that the whole of the primitive Church totally misunderstood him, this would not invalidate the recognition of the fact that the *bar naša* of whom Jesus spoke, is the Man of Dan. 7.13, to whom are given power, kingdom, and authority, and whom all peoples, nations, and tongues shall serve.

2. Moreover, the share of the Gentiles in the Kingdom of God is indirectly proclaimed by the way in which Jesus arranged his entry into Jerusalem (Mark 11.1–10 and parallels) in fulfilment of the saying in Zech. 9.9 about the King who is humble and, instead of a war-horse, chooses a he-ass[1] as his mount.[2] For this choice of a mount is in Zechariah immediately followed by the declaration, justifying that choice, that the coming King is the Prince of Peace for all nations: 'For he will[3] cut off the chariot from Ephraim, and the horse from Jerusalem, and the battle bow shall be cut off; and he shall speak peace unto the nations: and his dominion shall be from sea to sea, and from the River to the ends of the earth' (Zech. 9.10).

3. Next we must consider Mark 12.35–37, that frequently misunderstood saying about the Son of David. Here Jesus clearly intends to contrast the passages of Scripture which designate the Messiah as the Son of David with Ps. 110 which, in v.1, refers to

[1]L. Köhler, *Lexicon in Veteris Testamenti libros*, Leiden 1953, p. 702a, s.v. עַיִר.

[2]Rabbinic literature interprets Zech. 9.9 in a Messianic sense (for examples see Billerbeck I, pp. 842–4).

[3]Thus the LXX; Heb. text has 'I will'.

the Messiah as David's Lord. This pointing of the contrast should not be taken to mean that Jesus rejected the Davidic sonship, i.e the Messianic office, but we now know that here we have to do with a so-called Haggada question.[1] A Haggada question is one which indicates a contradiction in the Scriptures, to which the answer is regularly given: both passages of Scripture are right, but they refer to different points. In a similar way, in Mark 12.35–37, Jesus propounds a Haggada question arising from the contradiction between the designation of the Messiah as David's Son and as David's Lord, and suggests his answer thereto: both passages are right. The designation 'David's Son' refers to the earthly appearance of the hidden Messiah, while, on the other hand, he is David's Lord as the Enthroned One, that is to say, the one who is referred to in the following verse: 'Jahveh will send forth the rod of thy strength out of Zion' (Ps. 110.2).

4. But it is necessary above all to remember that Jesus thought of himself as the Servant of Jahveh.[2] Now it was written of the Servant of Jahveh that he would bring forth truth to the nations (Isa. 42.1, 4), that he was appointed to be a light to the nations (Isa. 42.6; 49.6; cf. Eth. Enoch 48.4; Luke 2.32), that he would sprinkle many nations (Isa. 52.15), and that he would bear the sins of many (Isa. 53.12).

All these four attributes of sovereignty imply, accordingly, that the Gentiles are included in Jesus' redemptive mission. The Scripture is fulfilled. Jesus dies for 'the many' (see p. 73 n. 1), and by word and deed declares that his lordship embraces the Gentile world. This promise for the Gentiles is wholly bound up with the fact that he is the fulfiller of Scripture.

But it must be said, finally, that the fulfilment goes beyond the Scripture. In Dan. 7.14 it is said of the Son of Man: 'All peoples, nations, and tongues shall serve him.' Jesus never affirmed this announcement. On the contrary, his word is: 'The Son of Man

---

[1]Pointed out by D. Daube, 'Four Types of Question', in *JTS*, N.S. 2, 1951, p. 48; reprinted in *The New Testament and Rabbinic Judaism*, London 1956, pp. 158–63, see p. 163.
[2]On the question of historicity see *TWNT* V, pp. 709–13; Eng. tr. in W. Zimmerli and J. Jeremias, *The Servant of God*², London 1965, pp. 99–106.

came not to be ministered unto'. He came to serve (Mark 10.45). Not only in his Passion is he the Servant of Jahveh; but also in exaltation, as Lord of all, he is still the one who came not to be served, but who girds himself and gives to his own the Bread and the Cup (Luke 12.37b).[1]

[1]Luke 12.37b in its present context is an allegorizing expansion of the parable of the servants who were commanded to watch (vv. 35–38); but the sentence is pre-Lucan, as may be seen from the ἀμήν, seldom used by Luke, and the Semitism of the redundant παρελθών, cf. J. Jeremias, *The Parables of Jesus*², p. 54 n. 18.

III

THE SOLUTION OF THE PROBLEM

Our study has landed us in what appears to be a complete contradiction. We have found, on the one hand, that Jesus limited his activity to Israel, and imposed the same limitation upon his disciples. On the other hand, it has been established that Jesus expressly promised the Gentiles a share in the Kingdom of God, and even warned his Jewish hearers that their own place might be taken by the Gentiles.

Help towards the resolution of the contradiction is provided by the logion in Matt. 8.11 f.:[1] 'I say unto you, they shall come in countless numbers[2] from the east and from the west, and may[3] sit down with Abraham, Isaac, and Jacob in the Kingdom of Heaven (v. 12) while the sons of the Kingdom will be cast out[4] into outer darkness; there shall be wailing and gnashing of teeth;' the parallel in Luke 13.28 f. has the concluding sentence reversed: 'then there will be wailing and gnashing of teeth, when you see Abraham, Isaac, and Jacob, and all the prophets in the Kingdom of God, but you yourselves cast out[5] (v. 29), while[6] they come

[1]H. Stoevesandt, *Jesus und die Heidenmission*, pp. 73 f.; cf. *TLZ* 74, 1949, col. 242.

[2]On πολλοί see below p. 73 n. 1. That in Matt. 8.11 πολλοί has an inclusive meaning is to be inferred from the connexion of that logion with the Old Testament passages relating to the eschatological pilgrimage of the nations (see below).

[3]The modal significance is characteristic of the Galilean-Aramaic imperfect, cf. W. B. Stevenson, *Grammar of Palestinian Jewish Aramaic*, Oxford 1924, §18.8.

[4]v.l. ἐξελεύσονται ℵ* syr.: Semitizing avoidance of the passive.

[5]Ὑμᾶς δὲ ἐκβαλλομένους ἔξω is an unfortunate rendering of an Aramaic circumstantial clause (cf. M. Black, *An Aramaic Approach to the Gospels and Acts²*, pp. 63 f.). What is wrong in the Greek rendering is: 1. the participle is made dependent on ὄψησθε (literally: 'when you see Abraham . . . and yourselves as cast out'), and 2. the secondary action ('see') has the finite verb, and the principal action ('cast out') the participle, instead of the reverse.

[6]Καί: Semitic parataxis in a logical hypotaxis.

from the east and the west, the north and the south, and sit down in the Kingdom of God.'

It is evident that this logion is early: (*a*) It represents a Jewish mode of thought (the patriarchs and prophets are mentioned; Jewish is the conception of future blessedness as sharing the Messianic banquet with the patriarchs; so, too, is the conception that the damned will see the blessed);[1] (*b*) the style is Semitic (e.g. antithetic parallelism in Matt., obtained by the contrasted pair ἔρχεσθαι and ἐκβάλλεσθαι; adverbial clause and parataxis in Luke);[2] (*c*) the language exhibits Semitisms (πολλοί in Matt. with inclusive meaning 'numberless'; ἡ βασιλεία τῶν οὐρανῶν in Matt.; οἱ υἱοὶ τῆς βασιλείας in Matt.; the article before κλαυθμός and βρυγμός in Matt. and Luke).

It is of decisive importance that we should understand clearly *when* the event envisaged in this warning is to take place. Two significant clues suggest the answer: 1. the patriarchs (Luke adds 'and all the prophets') are risen and seated as the most honoured guests at the banquet. 2. God pronounces the irrevocable sentence upon 'the sons of the Kingdom'. In other words: the gathering in of the Gentiles[3] occurs in the hour of the final judgement. Whither do they hasten from the ends of the earth? The Scripture tells us: to the Mountain of God. This is what Jesus read in his Bible: 'And it shall come to pass in the latter days, that the mountain of the Lord's house shall be established in the top of the mountains, and shall be exalted above the hills; and all nations shall flow únto it; and many peoples shall go and say, Come ye, and let us go up to the mountain of the Lord, to the house of the God of Jacob; and he will teach us of his ways, and we will walk in his paths' (Isa. 2.2 f., parallel in Micah 4.1 f.).[4]

[1] IV Ezra 7.38; Syr. Bar. 51.5 f.; for Rabbinic examples see Billerbeck II, p. 228; IV, pp. 1114 f. The same theme in connexion with the intermediate period occurs in IV Ezra 7.85; Luke 16.23.

[2] See p. 55 nn. 5 and 6.

[3] That it is the Gentiles who are indicated by πολλοί in Matt. 8.11 is shown by the fact that they are contrasted with the 'sons of the Kingdom', cf. Stoevesandt, op. cit. p. 73. Cf. also above p. 55 n. 2.

[4] The translations from the Old Testament follow the English R.V., except where the Zurich Bible, which, in its Old Testament part, is a masterpiece of scholarship, differs from it.

In attempting to draw a picture of what Jesus read in his Bible about the *eschatological pilgrimage of the Gentiles to the Mountain of God,* it must be emphasized at the outset that a true picture can only be arrived at by ignoring all the questions and conclusions of modern historical and literary criticism of the Old Testament, for such questions did not exist for Jesus. As we attempt to do this, five features emerge:

1. *The Epiphany of God.* The nations are expectant: 'The coast-lands shall wait for me, and on mine arm shall they trust' (Isa. 51.5). Now they hold their breath: 'Be silent, all flesh, before the Lord: for he is waked up out of his holy habitation' (Zech. 2.13). The epiphany of God will be visible. The Mountain of the Temple will rise above all mountains and hills (Isa. 2.2). The glory of God will be revealed to all the world (Isa. 40.5). God's truth will appear as a light of the nations (Isa. 51.4; 60.3); 'the Lord has made bare his holy arm in the eyes of all the nations' (Isa. 52.10). A Standard is displayed: 'In that day the Gentiles shall turn to the root of Jesse, which standeth as an ensign of the peoples (cf. 62.10), and his resting-place shall be glory' (11.10)— 'that is the Messiah' (Midr. Ps. 21, § 1).

2. *The Call of God.* God's epiphany is accompanied by his Word: 'God, even God the Lord hath spoken, and called the earth from the rising of the sun unto the going down thereof' (Ps. 50.1— Siphre Deut. § 343 on Ps. 50.2 adds 'in the days of the Messiah'). And this is the divine command addressed to the Gentiles who survive the final catastrophe: 'Assemble yourselves and come; draw near together, ye that are escaped of the nations . . . look unto me and be ye saved, all the ends of the earth: for I am God, and there is none else' (Isa. 45.20, 22). As God's instrument Israel echoes the call: 'Behold, thou shalt call a nation that thou knowest not, and a nation that knew not thee shall run unto thee, because of the Lord thy God, and for the Holy One of Israel; for he hath glorified thee' (Isa. 55.5). 'Declare his glory among the nations, his marvellous works among all the peoples . . . say among the nations, The Lord reigneth' (Ps. 96.3, 10). The Gentiles, too, who have survived the divine judgement,

proclaim the glory of God among the nations, and summon them to the pilgrimage to the Mountain of God (Isa. 66.19 f.). But God has yet another messenger, the Servant of the Lord, who not only restores the preserved of Israel, but whom God makes known as the light of the Gentiles (Isa. 42.6; 49.6). The response to the call is:

3. *The Journey of the Gentiles.* A road is constructed, a highway straight through the Near East, from Egypt and Assyria to Jerusalem (Isa. 19.23). At the same time the summons is heard in the cities of the Gentiles: 'Come ye, and let us go up to the mountain of the Lord' (Isa. 2.3). 'Let us go speedily to intreat the favour of the Lord, and to seek the Lord of hosts: I will go also' (Zech. 8.21). If there should happen to be a Jew of the Diaspora returning home, ten men out of all the languages of the nations will take hold of the skirt of his garment and say: 'We will go with you, for we have heard that God is with you' (v. 23). All the nations, led by their kings (Isa. 60.11; Ps. 47.10), stream towards Jerusalem, the throne of the Lord (Jer. 3.17), in an unending procession 'from sea to sea and from mountain to mountain' (Micah 7.12). Their shoulders are bent under the weight of the gifts which they bring (Isa. 18.7; Hag. 2.7; Ps. 68. 30, 32). The costly gifts which the nations bring are described in the vivid imagery of Isa. 60 (often quoted in Rabbinic literature), the wealth of the seas (v.5), gold, silver, and incense (vv. 6, 9), borne upon camels and dromedaries (v. 6); then come animal victims for sacrifice upon God's altar (v. 7), and costly wood from Lebanon for the building of the Temple (v. 13). They bear Israel's sons and daughters in their arms as a precious treasure (v. 6), 'upon horses, and in chariots, and in litters, and upon mules and upon dromedaries, to my holy mountain Jerusalem, saith the Lord' (Isa. 66.20). The gates are to be kept open day and night, 'that men may bring unto thee the wealth of the nations' (60.11). Those wh o are left out of all the nations come year by year to the feast of tabernacles in Jerusalem to worship (Zech. 14.16), even new moon after new moon they come, sabbath after sabbath (Isa. 66.18). 'They shall come trembling out of their close places' (Micah 7.17), bowing down (Isa. 60.14). The goal of the pilgrimage is:

4. *Worship at the World-sanctuary*. 'Even them [the strangers that join themselves to the Lord] will I bring to my holy mountain, and make them joyful in my house of prayer; their burnt offerings and their sacrifices shall be accepted upon mine altar: for mine house shall be called a house of prayer for all peoples' (Isa. 56.7; Mark 11.17). All the ends of the earth shall turn to the Lord (Ps. 22.28); they see the glory of God (Isa. 66.18) and fall on their knees before him (Isa. 45.23) in the courts of the World-sanctuary (Ps. 96.8). Moreover, God will cleanse their lips: 'For then will I turn to the people a pure language (Heb. "lip") that they may all call upon the name of the Lord' (Zeph. 3.9). With cleansed lips they will confess: 'Our fathers have inherited nought but lies, even vanity and things wherein there is no profit' (Jer. 16.19), and add their tribute of praise: 'For thou art great and doest wondrous things, thou art God alone' (Ps. 86.10); 'only in the Lord is righteousness and strength' (Isa. 45.24). A touching description of this act of adoration is given in Isa. 45.14. The Sabaean prisoners of war will be brought in chains by the Persians to Jerusalem, praying as they pass: 'And the Sabaeans, men of stature, shall pass before thee in chains and fall down before thee, and make supplication to thee, saying, Surely God is in thee, and there is none else, there is no God.'[1] The worship addressed to God is accompanied by lowly homage to the Messianic king (Ps. 72.9–11), and to the people of God (Isa. 49.23), bearers of blessing for the world (Isa. 19.24). The divine response to the adoration of the Gentiles is expressed in the amazing blessing, transcending all national boundaries:

'Blessed be Egypt, my people,
    Assyria, the work of my hands,
        and Israel, mine inheritance' (Isa. 19.25).

5. *The Messianic Banquet on the World-mountain*. The truth that the Gentiles now belong to the people of God,[2] to the peaceful reign

[1]This is the rendering of this ambiguous text advocated by K. Budde (in E. Kautzsch, *Die Heilige Schrift des A.T.*, *I*[4], Tübingen 1922, p. 672).
[2]'Many nations shall become his people, and he will dwell in the midst of them' (Zech. 2.11); 'the princes of the peoples are gathered together to be the people of the God of Abraham' (Ps. 47.9).

of the Messiah over the nations (Zech. 9.10), and to the dominion of the Son of Man (Dan. 7.14), receives its visible expression in the festal banquet of the nations upon the Mountain of God. 'And in this mountain shall the Lord of hosts make unto all peoples a feast of fat things, a feast of wines on the lees, of fat things full of marrow, of wines on the lees well refined. And he will destroy in this mountain the face of the covering that is cast over all peoples, and the veil that is spread over all nations. He will destroy death for ever' (Isa. 25.6–8). That the act of eating and drinking may mediate the vision of God, is an ancient element of biblical symbolism which runs through the whole Bible from beginning (Gen. 3.22) to end (Rev. 22.17), and which is of fundamental importance for the understanding of all the statements in apocalyptic literature and in the New Testament about the festal banquet of the Messianic age.[1] Moreover this conception is stressed in the passage before us in the promise that when the festal meal on the Mountain of God is celebrated, the veil that covers the eyes of the Gentiles will be for ever rent asunder, and they will behold God with unveiled face.

In all the passages of the Old Testament, without exception, in which reference is made to the eschatological pilgrimage of the Gentiles, the goal of the pilgrimage is the scene of God's revelation of himself, Zion, the holy Mountain of God. From this it is to be inferred that the movement is always thought of as 'centripetal';[2] the Gentiles will not be evangelized where they dwell, but will be summoned to the holy Mount by the divine epiphany. Zion is always the appointed centre for their gathering. The redemption celebrated at the festal meal is the redemption of Israel, revealed to the astonished Gentiles. The fact is that wherever the Old Testament is concerned with the redemption of the Gentiles, it guarantees them a share in the revelation vouchsafed to Israel, and inclusion in God's redeemed community.[3]

[1] I have given numerous examples in *The Eucharistic Words of Jesus*[2], pp. 233–6.

[2] B. Sundkler, 'Jésus et les païens', pp. 28, 31 f.; S. Aalen, *Die Begriffe 'Licht' und 'Finsternis'*, pp. 204 f., 209, 212 ff., 228, 301 f.

[3] This is why it says in Matt. 3.9, parallel Luke 3.8, that God can raise up

The conception of the pilgrimage of the Gentiles is also to be found in the extra-canonical literature. It has repeatedly been inserted into the text of the Septuagint (LXX Isa. 54.15; Amos 9.12 = Acts 15.17).[1] The worship of the nations at the central sanctuary is a constantly recurring theme of the eschatological expectation: Tobit 13.13; Orac. Sib. III 716 ff., 725 f., 772–5; Test. Ben. 9.2 (see below p. 64); Eth. En. 10.21; 48.5; 90.33; Syr. Bar. 68.5.[2] Another favourite theme is that of the gifts which the Gentiles bring as tokens of their submission. 'Rejoice greatly, O Zion! Break forth into song, O Jerusalem! Be glad, all ye cities of Judah! Let your gates stand open, that the Gentiles may come in to you, and that their kings may serve you,' a quotation from the newly discovered Palestinian texts,[3] cf. also Tobit 13.13; Orac. Sib. III 772 f.; Eth. En. 53.1; Ps..Sol. 17.31; IV Ezra 13.13; Rev. 21.26 and the rabbinic literature.[4] The beneficent activity of the Messiah is frequently stressed: the Gentiles are attracted by the revelation of his dominion and power (Ps. Sol. 17.31, cf. IV Ezra 13.12 f.);[5] he reveals to them 'the new knowledge' (Test. Ben. 11.2, cf. Test. Levi 18.9). Nevertheless, so far as the rabbinic literature is concerned, it must once more[6] be emphasized that such universalistic conceptions are of rare occurrence; the exclusively nationalistic conception of the Messianic age which envisaged the destruction of the Gentiles had completely prevailed

---

children to Abraham (not 'to himself') from the stones, and in Matt. 8.11 that the Gentiles sit at table with the patriarchs (not with God). The eschatological divine community is 'rooted in history, in the community of the people of God' (A. Oepke, *Das neue Gottesvolk*, Gütersloh 1950, p. 157).

[1]LXX Deut. 32.43 should also be understood in this sense (cf. *B.M.* Βέλλας, 'Τὰ χωρία Δευτ. 32.43 καὶ Ζαχ. 14.17', Θεολογία 13, 1935, pp. 137–45), so too LXX Isa. 41.25.

[2]Rabbinic examples in Billerbeck III, pp. 150–2.

[3]IQM 12.13 f. par. 19.5 f.

[4]Billerbeck IV, pp. 883, 908, 938 *et al.*; Targ. Isa. 16.1.

[5]Cf. also Eth. En. 90.37. For Rabbinic examples see Billerbeck III, pp. 148, 150, 153; IV, pp. 896, 908, 938 *et al.*; Targ. Isa. 16.1. Rabbinic examples of the conception that the Light of God, of the Messiah, of Jerusalem, of Israel, of the redemption, attracts the Gentiles, have been collected by S. Aalen, op. cit. pp. 299 ff.

[6]See above pp. 40 f.

after the destruction of the Temple in A.D. 70.[1] But, altogether apart from the fact that the destruction of Jerusalem in A.D. 70 and its effects lie outside the chronological limits of this study, it is unnecessary for our purpose to enter into the details of the treatment in the rabbinical literature of the conception of the eschatological pilgrimage of the Gentiles, since Jesus was not influenced by late Jewish exegesis, but by the Old Testament itself.[2] The point may be illustrated by two examples: Mal. 1.11 ('From the rising of the sun even unto the going down of the same my name is great among the Gentiles') is interpreted by the rabbinic literature as referring to the Torah and the evening prayer,[3] while Jesus, on the other hand, as may be seen from Matt. 8.11, interprets it of the eschatological ingathering of the Gentiles. Again, the rabbinic literature refers Isa. 25.6 ('And in this mountain shall the Lord of hosts make unto all peoples a feast of fat things, a feast of wines on the lees') to the cup of wrath which the Gentiles are to drink,[4] or to the shame and bitter sufferings which they are to undergo,[5] whereas Jesus, in accordance with the meaning of the text, interprets the passage as referring to the Gentiles' share in the salvation of the Messianic age (Matt. 8.11).

Returning, then, to the message of Jesus, it should now be clear that in Matt. 8.11 and its parallel in Luke 13.29 we have a succinct summary of the Old Testament utterances concerning the eschatological pilgrimage of the Gentiles to the Mount of God at the time of the Last Judgement. This saying of Jesus has special reference to two Old Testament passages: 1. to Isa. 49.12, 'Lo, these shall come from far: and, lo, these from the north and from the west,'[6] and 2. to Isa. 25.6 f., where it speaks of the feast which the Lord of hosts has prepared for all peoples on his holy mountain. As we have already seen on pp. 59 f., the sacred meal mediates God's redeeming activity. The nature of the special redemptive grace in

[1] Billerbeck III, pp. 144 f.
[2] Cf. H. Stoevesandt, *Jesus und die Heidenmission*, p. 145.
[3] Billerbeck III, pp. 152 f.
[4] Siphre Deut. 324 on Deut. 32.34.
[5] Targ. Isa. 25.6.
[6] Jesus interpreted the passage as referring to the Gentiles (G. Stählin, in *EMZ* 7, 1950, p. 105).

which the Gentiles participate is shown by the fact that Matt. 8.11 speaks of their sitting at table with the patriarchs. Abraham, Isaac, and Jacob are designated as the three pillars which support the world;[1] they represent the people of God. The fact that the Gentiles participate with the patriarchs in the Messianic feast indicates that they have been incorporated into the people of God at the consummation of all things. They stand on an equal footing, and to sit at table with them no longer causes defilement;[2] earthly distinctions have disappeared. They drink of the water of life, and their hunger is appeased by the vision of the Shechinah.[3]

It is from this point of view that we not only may but must interpret all the parables and sayings of Jesus which speak of the eschatological banquet. The Messianic feast of which Jesus speaks so often and under so many symbols as the wedding feast, as the high festival which awaits the faithful and wise servant,[4] as the final Passover,[5] as the satisfying of all hunger,[6] is none other than the feast upon Mount Zion described in Isa. 25.6 f., God's universal feast towards which the nations flow, where the veil that shrouds them, and the covering that blinds their eyes, shall be rent asunder.

The reference in Matt. 8.11 to the Gentiles' participation with Abraham in the Messianic banquet throws light on the saying in John 8.56. When the Johannine gospel makes Jesus say that Abraham rejoiced to see his day, this ἐχάρη embraces Abraham's joy in the coming fulfilment of the promise given to him that he should be 'the father of countless nations' (Gen. 17.4; Rom. 4.17).

The conception of the pilgrimage of the Gentiles is not confined to Matt. 8.11 in the gospels, but finds frequent expression in the sayings of Jesus. In addition to the picture of the universal Messianic banquet we find a whole series of metaphors representing

[1] Midr. Ps. 1 §15.
[2] Acts 10.28; 11.1 ff. (On the question of the defilement attributed to the Gentiles from the end of the first century B.C. see J. Jeremias, *Infant Baptism in the First Four Centuries*, London 1960, pp. 25–8.)
[3] Thus Midr. Ps. 45 §3, concerning the righteous.
[4] Matt. 25.21, 23: χαρά = חֶדְוְתָא = 'festival'.
[5] Luke 22.16.
[6] Matt. 5.6, parallel Luke 6.21.

the ingathering of the Gentiles. We read in Matt. 25.31 f. that at the Parousia God[1] will gather all nations before the throne of the Son of Man (συναχθήσονται ἔμπροσθεν αὐτοῦ πάντα τὰ ἔθνη). The verb συνάγεσθαι is here an eschatological technical term, as, for example, may be seen from Test. Ben. 9.2, where it is used in connexion with the final Temple: καὶ συναχθήσονται ἐκεῖ αἱ δώδεκα φυλαὶ καὶ πάντα τὰ ἔθνη (the verbal agreement with Matt. 25.32: συναχθήσονται . . . πάντα τὰ ἔθνη calls for notice).[2] The expression συνάγειν is drawn from the shepherd's usage, as may be inferred from the continuation of Matt. 25.32, where the nations are depicted as a flock or, more precisely, as a mixed flock of white sheep and black goats (not he-goats), as is customary in Palestine.[3] *The eschatological gathering of the flock* always presupposes its scattering, cf. John 11.51 f., ὅτι ἔμελλεν Ἰησοῦς ἀποθνήσκειν ὑπὲρ τοῦ ἔθνους, καὶ οὐχ ὑπὲρ τοῦ ἔθνους μόνον, ἀλλ' ἵνα καὶ τὰ τέκνα τοῦ θεοῦ τὰ διεσκορπισμένα συναγάγῃ εἰς ἕν. The contrasting verb (δια-) σκορπίζειν is, like συνάγειν, also an eschatological technical term. It indicates the time of tribulation before the end: πατάξω τὸν ποιμένα καὶ τὰ πρόβατα διασκορπισθήσονται (Mark 14.27 and parallels).[4]

The gathering of the scattered, shepherdless and helpless flock is a symbol of approaching redemption and an essential element in Israel's hope of the future; every day the synagogue prays (in the tenth benediction of the Eighteen Benedictions) for the gathering of the banished ones; similarly the Church prays for the eschatological gathering of her scattered members into the Kingdom from the four winds (*Didache* 10.5). In John 11.51 f., as also in Test. Ben. 9.2 and Matt. 25.32, the picture of the scattered flock is extended to the Gentile world; they too belong to the flock for whose gathering together Jesus dies. It can be seen from Test. Ben. 9.2 (see above p. 61) that the gathering of the scattered nations will take place at the new Temple of God on Mount Zion. Instead

[1]The passive συναχθήσονται is a circumlocution for the divine activity which is here conceived as mediated through an angel (Mark 13.27 and parallels).

[2]Cf. Tobit 13.15 AB συναχθήσονται (the sons of the righteous) καὶ εὐλογήσουσιν τὸν κύριον τῶν δικαίων.

[3]J. Jeremias, *The Parables of Jesus*[2], p. 206.

[4]Cf. John 10.12; 16.32.

of the compound verb συνάγειν John 10.16 has the simple ἄγειν for the eschatological gathering of the flock from the nations. The ἀγαγεῖν (John 10.16) of the 'other sheep' takes place through Jesus' calling them; they hear his voice and come streaming into the sheep-fold—'and there shall be one flock and one shepherd'. In Matt. 25.32, John 10.16 and 11.51 f. we have the same picture: the scattered Gentile flock is brought to Zion by God's shepherd and united with the flock of God's people.

In the previous section mention has been made of a third symbol of the eschatological pilgrimage of the Gentiles, namely, the *Temple of the New Age*. More than once does Jesus speak of the eschatological sanctuary; it will be erected in three days after the destruction of the old Temple (Mark 14.58 and parallels), Peter is its foundation stone (Matt. 16.18), the Son of Man is the stone that completes the building (Mark 12.10 and parallels). Thus constituted, the new Temple is always the universal sanctuary where the Gentiles too may worship; thus did Jesus read in his Bible,[1] and thus did the apocalyptists teach.[2] The story of the cleansing of the Temple shows that Jesus shared this universalistic view of the eschatological Temple. It is possible, though of this I am not certain, to see a deeper meaning in the fact that it was actually the court of the Gentiles that he cleansed.[3] In any case it is certain that the passage of Scripture upon which Jesus based his action refers to the Gentiles: ὁ οἶκός μου οἶκος προσευχῆς κληθήσεται πᾶσιν τοῖς ἔθνεσιν (Mark 11.17 = Isa. 56.7, for the context see above p. 59).[4] Jesus explicitly states that he is preparing a place of worship for the

[1]See above p. 59.
[2]See above p. 61, cf. also p. 64 (Test. Ben. 9.2). As an example see also Eth. En. 90.33: 'And all that had been destroyed and dispersed, and all the beasts of the field, and all the birds of the heaven, assembled in that house.'
[3]In my judgement E. Lohmeyer lays too much emphasis on this point in 'Die Reinigung des Tempels', in *TB* 20, 1941, pp. 257 ff.; *Kultus und Evangelium*, Göttingen 1942, pp. 44 ff. That Jesus cleansed the court of the Gentiles is due in the first place to the fact that it was there that the money changers set up their tables three weeks before the Passover, when the Temple tax fell due (Sheq. 1.3, hence not throughout the whole year).
[4]It is not necessary to regard the absence of the last three words from Matthew (21.13) and Luke (19.46) as a reflection of the destruction of the Temple in A.D. 70; it may simply represent an abbreviated quotation.

Gentiles. The eschatological moment has arrived;[1] the profaned sanctuary is to be cleansed;[2] God is coming to his Temple. This is the point where the restoration of Israel begins, to be completed when the nations throng to worship[3] in God's House whose gates stand open day and night.[4] Again John agrees with the Synoptists when he makes Jesus speak to the Samaritan woman of the hour when national and ecclesiastical differences between Israel and the Gentiles will be removed, and there will be only one community which will worship the Father in spirit and in truth (John 4.21, 23). The same theme appears in John 12.20 ff. The *Ἕλληνες* who have come on pilgrimage to Jerusalem, and seek to see Jesus, are for him the representatives of the whole Gentile world which, after his death and resurrection, would throng hither to worship (v. 23, see pp. 37 f.). As such they are, in Bengel's appropriate words, *praeludium regni Dei*.

The same thought is expressed by Jesus in ever fresh images, as, for example, in Matt. 5.14. G. von Rad has shown that 'the city set on a hill' that cannot be hid is the *city of God on the world-mountain*.[5] Only by this interpretation is the full force of the word 'cannot' (οὐ δύναται) brought out: it is unthinkable that the glory (*kabhodh*) of the city of God should remain hidden. Once again the thought of the ingathering of the Gentiles makes its appearance; for in the Old Testament and in late Jewish literature the idea persistently and repeatedly recurs that it is the light of the city of God, the bright beam of the *kabhodh*, which is the signal for the eschatological pilgrimage of the nations.[6] Closely connected with Matt.

---

[1] Κληθήσεται is an eschatological future.

[2] J. Jeremias, *Jesus als Weltvollender*, Gütersloh 1930, pp. 35–44.

[3] A. Cole has rightly said in *The New Temple*, London 1950, p. 31, 'The two issues, abolition of the old material Temple and inclusion of the Gentiles, are closely linked both in the Sayings of Jesus and the later Catechesis of the Church, so that the two problems are fundamentally one and the same.' In primitive Christian eschatology the restoration of the Temple and the pilgrimage of the Gentiles are inseparably linked together, as may be seen for example in Acts 15.16 f., cf. Rev. 21.22 ff.

[4] Cf. Isa. 60.11; IQM 12.13 f.; 19.5 f. (see above p. 21 n. 2); Rev. 21.25.

[5] 'Die Stadt auf dem Berge', in *Ev.Th.* 8, 1948/9, pp. 439–47.

[6] There is a comprehensive collection of material in S. Aalen, *Die Begriffe 'Licht' und 'Finsternis'*.

5.14 is the saying about the lamp which is not to be placed under a bushel (i.e. which should not be extinguished),[1] but which should be placed on the lamp-stand (Mark 4.21; Matt. 5.15; Luke 8.16; 11.33). The context shows that the saying has been variously interpreted by the evangelists,[2] but in any case it implies the comparison of the activity of Jesus with the shining forth of the *eschatological light*,[3] i.e. with the light of the revelation of God which summons the nations to Zion. This is apparently Luke's intention in adding to the twice repeated saying in each case the words: ἵνα οἱ εἰσπορευόμενοι βλέπωσιν τὸ φῶς (Luke 8.16; 11.33).[4]

We see the same universal character as that of the eschatological light in the *river of life,* which flows from the sacred rock and satisfies the thirst, first of Israel, then of the whole world.[5] According to Zech. 14.16, the survivors of all the nations will come up yearly to the Mount of God to keep the feast of Tabernacles, whose whole ritual has as its object the prayer for rain for the coming year;[6] 'and it shall be that whoso of all the families of the earth goeth not up to Jerusalem to worship the King, the Lord of hosts, upon them there shall be no rain' (v. 17). On either side of the river of water of life flowing from beneath the throne of God and the Lamb (Rev. 22.1), there grow the trees of life whose leaves are for 'the healing of the nations' (v. 2). According to John 7.37 f., at the feast of Tabernacles Jesus, referring to himself as the true Rock from which would flow the water of life for the world,[7] cried: 'If any man thirst, let him come unto me, and drink, he that believeth on me'; hence this Johannine proclamation of salvation implies the conception of the eschatological pilgrimage of the Gentiles.[8]

[1] J. Jeremias, 'Die Lampe unter dem Scheffel', in *ZNTW* 39, 1940, pp. 237–40, reprinted in J. Jeremias, *Abba*, Göttingen 1966, pp. 99–102.
[2] In Matt. 5.15 the light is interpreted of the disciples, in Mark 4.21 of the gospel, and in Luke 11.33 either of Jesus himself (cf. 11.29–32) or of the inner light (cf. 11.34–36).
[3] J. Jeremias, *The Parables of Jesus*², pp. 120 f.
[4] Ibid. p. 38. Cf. John 8.12: ἐγώ εἰμι τὸ φῶς τοῦ κόσμου.
[5] J. Jeremias, *Golgotha* (=Angelos Beih. 1), Leipzig 1926, pp. 54–58, 60–64, 82–85.
[6] Ibid. pp. 60 ff.
[7] J. Jeremias, *Jesus als Weltvollender*, p. 49. Cf. John 4.14; I Cor. 10.4.
[8] Cf. B. Sundkler, 'Jésus et les païens', pp. 31 f.

Another image which calls for notice is that of the *inheritance*. The verb κληρονομεῖν had become an eschatological technical term in late Jewish literature,.implying a share in the coming Kingdom.[1] Jesus always uses κληρονομεῖν in this sense, and no doubt in Matt. 25.34 he is referring to the Gentiles: 'Come, ye blessed of my Father, inherit the kingdom prepared for you from the foundation of the world'.[2] Hence the metaphor 'inheritance' carries with it the assurance to the Gentiles of their participation in the world to come, for the realization of which they are gathered before the throne of the Kingdom (v. 32), and no doubt this holds good for all the passages where Jesus uses the word κληρονομεῖν, for there is only one inheritance.

From the fact that in Ethiopic Enoch (39.8; 71.16)[3] the words 'inheritance' and 'dwelling' occur in parallelism it may be inferred that the 'many abodes' of which John 14.2 speaks, are to be understood in the same universalistic sense as κληρονομεῖν in the synoptic gospels.

Inseparable from the eschatological inheritance is the *joy of the Messianic Age*, described in Matt. 25.21, 23 as a glad festival (cf. p. 63 n. 4), in Luke 15.7, 10 as the joy of God, in John 4.36 as the joy shared by both sowers and reapers, and in John 15.11; 16.24; 17.13 as joy fulfilled (=*simkha šelema*=the joy of the Messianic Age).[4] The epithet οἱ εὐλογημένοι τοῦ πατρός μου (Matt. 25.34) indicates the righteous among the Gentiles as sharers in this fulness of joy.

In the parable of the grain of mustard seed the manifestation of the Kingdom is compared to a tall shrub (so Mark 4.32; δένδρον: Matt. 13.32, parallel Luke 13.19), 'which putteth out great branches, so that *the birds of heaven* can lodge under the shadow thereof (κατασκηνοῦν)' (Mark 4.32 and parallels). The tree which provides shelter for the birds is already in the Old Testament a common figure for a mighty kingdom which protects its dependent states (Ezek. 17.23; 31.6; Dan. 4.9, 11, 18). 'The birds of the

---

[1] W. Foerster, *TWNT* III, pp. 779 ff.
[2] The passive is a circumlocution for the divine name.
[3] W. Foerster, *TWNT* III, p. 780. 40 f.
[4] Billerbeck II, pp. 429 f., 566.

heaven . . . are the Gentiles', according to the Midrashic literature.[1] Moreover the verb κατασκηνοῦν, which, like the simple form
σκηνοῦν, is often used as an eschatological technical term, is
applied in the *Book of Asenath* to the Gentiles' seeking refuge in
the eschatological city of God: 'Thy name will be "City of
Refuge"; for in thee many Gentiles will seek refuge (ἐν σοὶ
καταφεύξονται ἔθνη πολλά) and under thy wings they will dwell
(κατασκηνώσουσιν), and many Gentiles will find protection in thee.'[2]
The parable of the mustard seed, then, is another expression of the
conception of the eschatological pilgrimage of the Gentiles when
it speaks of the host of birds which nest in the shelter of the
mustard bush.

If we have correctly interpreted Mark 14.9 and Matt. 24.14
(see pp. 22 ff.), the passive κηρύσσεσθαι, used in both these passages
as a circumlocution for the divine name, implies the *eschatological
angelic summons* (cf. Rev. 14.6 f.). In the last day the ultimate
victory of God will be proclaimed by an angelic voice to the
nations of the world (Matt. 24.14: εἰς μαρτύριον πᾶσιν τοῖς ἔθνεσιν;
Mark 14.9: εἰς ὅλον τὸν κόσμον, where the εἰς renders an Aramaic
lᵉ, which refers to the hearers of the message, see above p. 22 n.2).
The same conception of the angelic summons is to be found in
the expression συναχθήσονται in Matt. 25.32 (cf. Mark 13.27:
ἀποστελεῖ τοὺς ἀγγέλους καὶ ἐπισυνάξει τοὺς ἐκλεκτούς), similarly applied to the nations. The proclamation of the ushering in of the
final act by the mouth of the divine messenger gives the signal to
the nations for the eschatological pilgrimage.

The angels who announce the coming of the end are part of the
angelic train of the Son of Man (Mark 8.38 and parallels; 13.27 and
parallels; Matt. 25.31); they are, like the Son of Man's throne
(Matt. 19.28; 25.31, cf. Mark 14.62 and parallels), visible mani-
festations of his δύναμις (Mark 13.26 and parallels), of his δόξα
(Mark 8.38 and parallels; 10.37; 13.26 and parallels; Matt. 19.28;
25.31), and of his βασιλεία (Matt. 16.28; 20.21; Luke 22.29). All

[1]Midr. Ps. 104 §13 on Ps. 104.12; cf. Eth. En. 90.33 (quoted above p. 65
n. 2); b. Aboda Zara 41a. The comparison of the Gentiles with the birds in
j. Abod. Z. III, 42c. 44; Num. R. 13 on Num. 7.13 is based on Isa. 10.14.
[2]Chap. 15, ed. Batiffol, p.61. 9 ff.

the above passages, without exception, have their source in Dan. 7.14,[1] where it is said of the Son of Man that power, honour, and dominion are given to him, in order that 'all peoples, nations and tongues shall serve him'. Wherever Jesus speaks of the *power, dominion and kingdom of the returning Son of Man,* the Gentile world is therefore included.

One last example is of special importance. In Matt. 5.35 Jesus prohibits swearing by Jerusalem ὅτι πόλις ἐστὶν τοῦ μεγάλου βασιλέως. The title of 'the Great King' applied to God comes from the Old Testament where it occurs four times (Mal. 1.14; Ps. 47.2; 48.2; 95.3); in all four places it designates God as Lord of the world, to whom pertains dominion over all nations. The expression 'the city of the Great King' shows that Matt. 5.34 is a quotation from Ps. 48.1, 2: '. . . his holy mountain, beautiful in elevation, the joy of the whole earth, is mount Zion, on the sides of the north, the city of the great King'. Jesus therefore forbids his disciples to swear by Jerusalem, because Mount Zion bears the city of the Lord of the nations,[2] whose majesty may not be insulted by casual oaths sworn by the place of his throne. The fact that the title 'the Great King' applied to God in Matt. 5.35 expresses the universality of the rule of God assumes an even greater importance, because it proves that the expression βασιλεία τῶν οὐρανῶν or βασιλεία τοῦ θεοῦ, in *all* the numerous passages where Jesus uses this central conception of his proclamation, *includes the Gentile world.* Recognition of this fact is confirmed by the statement in Matt. 25.34 that God has prepared the kingdom from the foundation of the world for the righteous from among the nations.

Thus we see that the incorporation of the Gentiles in the Kingdom of God promised by the prophets, was expected and announced by Jesus as God's *eschatological act of power, as the great final manifestation of God's free grace.* For the last time God brings life out of death, creates children to Abraham out of stones, when in the hour of final revelation he summons the nations to

[1] J. W. Doeve, *Jewish Hermeneutics in the Synoptic Gospels and Acts,* Assen 1954, pp. 149 ff.

[2] For Rabbinic examples of Jerusalem as the future metropolis of the world see: Midr. Ps. 36 §6; Midr. Cant. 1.5.

Zion, and by constituting the universal people of God from Jews and Gentiles abolishes all earthly distinctions.

By establishing the fact that Jesus expected the incorporation of the Gentiles into the people of God as the result of God's eschatological act of power, we have resolved the apparent contradiction, to wit, that, on the one hand, Jesus limited his activity to Israel, and during his lifetime forbade his disciples to overstep the boundaries of Israel, while, on the other hand, he promised the Gentiles a permanent and unrestricted part in the Kingdom of God: we have to do with two successive events, first the call to Israel, and subsequently the redemptive incorporation of the Gentiles in the Kingdom of God. Moreover, the attitude of the primitive community towards the Gentiles appears under a new light. We shall see shortly that it was not particularistic narrowness that caused the primitive community to address their first preaching to Israel, but in so doing they were guided by the same attitude as Jesus towards the redemptive mission, and like Jesus expected the universal Kingdom of God as the final consummation.

The only question now remaining is: why did Jesus draw so sharp a distinction between his present mission to Israel and God's final summons to the Gentiles? Why did he avoid as far as possible any anticipation of the final crisis? Why did he confine the summons to the Gentiles so exclusively to God? Since Jesus himself gives no direct answer to these questions, we shall do well to examine first the answer given by the primitive Church. Its tenor is that two prior conditions must be fulfilled before God's call could go out to the Gentiles:

1. The promise of salvation given to 'the fathers' (Rom. 15.8), and to 'the sons of the prophets and of the covenant' (Acts 3.25), must first be fulfilled, the children must first be fed, before the incorporation of the Gentiles into the people of God could be effected. This is the universal conviction of the earliest Christianity. Not only in Paul's writings do we find the statement 'to the Jew first' (Rom. 1.16; 2.9, 10), but also in Acts 3.26 ($\dot{\upsilon}\mu\hat{\iota}\nu\ \pi\rho\hat{\omega}\tau o\nu$); 13.46 ($\dot{\upsilon}\mu\hat{\iota}\nu\ \mathring{\eta}\nu\ \mathring{\alpha}\nu\alpha\gamma\kappa\alpha\hat{\iota}o\nu\ \pi\rho\hat{\omega}\tau o\nu\ \lambda\alpha\lambda\eta\theta\hat{\eta}\nu\alpha\iota\ \tau\grave{o}\nu\ \lambda\acute{o}\gamma o\nu\ \tauο\hat{\upsilon}\ \theta\epsilon o\hat{\upsilon}$), and Mark

71

7.27 (ἄφες πρῶτον χορτασθῆναι τὰ τέκνα);[1] the word 'to the Jew first' is borne out by the fact that Paul, according to the account in Acts, invariably addressed himself first to the synagogues, and the First Epistle to the Corinthians makes it clear that the earliest strand of the Corinthian church was composed of Jewish Christians. The restoration of 'the tabernacle of David that is fallen' is, according to Acts 15.16 f. (=Amos 9.11 f. LXX), the preliminary to the turning of the Gentiles to the Lord.[2] We have evidence in Matt. 10.5 f. for the conclusion that this primitive 'to the Jew first', borne witness to by the early Church, which expresses the conviction that the offer of the gospel to Israel must necessarily precede the incorporation of the Gentiles into the Kingdom of God, goes back to Jesus himself. The prohibition in Matt. 10.5 f.:

> 'Go not to the Gentiles
> and enter not the province of Samaria,
>   but go rather to the lost sheep of the house of Israel'

seems to militate against a contrary view.[3] The opinion had evidently obtained currency among the disciples that the eschatological hour had already arrived, and that the Kingdom of God must be proclaimed to the whole world. Jesus' refusal made it clear that the last hour had not yet arrived; the message of salvation must first be addressed to Israel.

2. The second prior condition which must be fulfilled before the dawn of God's eschatological day could break is most clearly indicated in the gospel of John, where, as was pointed out on pp. 37 f., the fact is repeatedly emphasized that the time of the Gentiles must follow the Cross. The words of Jesus at the Last Supper make it clear that this was in the mind of Jesus. The blood of the true passover Lamb must first be shed 'for many' (Mark

---

[1] J. Munck, *Paul and the Salvation of Mankind*, p. 261.

[2] It is true that Paul in Rom. 11.25 f. has the reverse order: the πλήρωμα τῶν ἐθνῶν will be saved first, and subsequently πᾶς Ἰσραήλ. Paul calls this insight which, according to Rom. 11.11, has been mediated to him through the word παραζηλοῦν ('to make jealous', Deut. 32.21), a 'mystery' (v. 25). As Israel refused to accept the gospel God decided to reverse the order of salvation and to provoke Israel to jealousy through the repentance of the Gentiles. But this lies outside the limits of our study.

[3] J. Munck, op. cit. p. 259.

14.24), the ransom must be paid 'for many' (Mark 10.45), namely, for the countless hosts from all nations (Isa. 53.11 f.),[1] before the universal Kingdom of God could arrive.

Jesus realized that it was his earthly task to prepare for the hour of the revelation of the Kingdom by fulfilling these two necessary preconditions. 'The reason why Jesus came to Israel was precisely because his mission concerned the whole world.'[2] That is to say, his announcement of salvation to Israel, just as much as his vicarious death, was at the same time an act of service to the Gentiles. Both took place *in order that* the incorporation of the Gentiles into the Kingdom of God might be possible. Jesus' preaching to Israel was the precondition, his death for countless hosts rendered possible, and his parousia will bring into being, the people of God of the New Age, and the Kingdom of God over the whole world.

---

[1]On the Semitizing inclusive use of πολλοί in both these passages with the meaning of 'a great multitude, a countless number', see J. Jeremias, *The Eucharistic Words of Jesus*[2], pp. 179–182, 226–231, and the art. πολλοί in *TWNT* VI, pp. 536–45. On the question whether Jesus recognized himself as the Servant of Jahveh in Isa. 53, cf. *The Servant of God*[2], pp. 99–106. On the early date of Mark 10.45 (also as compared with Luke 22.27), cf. J. Jeremias, 'Das Lösegeld für Viele (Mk. 10.45)', in *Judaica* 3, 1947–48, pp. 249–64, reprinted in J. Jeremias, *Abba*, Göttingen 1966, pp. 216–29.

[2]J. Munck, op. cit. p. 266.

IV

CONCLUSION

WHAT ABOUT THE MISSION?

WHAT conclusions for the modern missionary task may be drawn from the strictly eschatological outlook of Jesus? Has it been rendered superfluous by acceptance of the fact that according to the preaching of Jesus it will be by God's act of power that the Gentiles will be brought in to the Kingdom of God in the final consummation? Far from it. What is significant for the missionary task is the realization to which we have been brought, that it is firmly rooted in God's redemptive activity. In Jesus' sayings about the Gentiles we find: 1. an unparalleled insistence on humility. Man can do nothing. It is not our preaching that brings about the ingathering of the Gentiles. *Even Jesus himself did not make the world Christian, but he died on the Cross.* God alone does it all. The fundamental note and inmost core of the message of Jesus, resounding in all his sayings about the Gentiles, is confidence in the reality of God and the vastness of his mercy.[1]

But at the same time the sayings of Jesus about the Gentiles are: 2. a revelation of the overriding importance and value of the missionary task. Easter saw the dawn of the Last Day. The Gentile mission is the beginning of God's final act in the gathering of the Gentiles. The Gentile mission is God's own activity. As God's eschatological activity it is an anticipation of the visible enthronement of the Son of Man, and as such it is 'the actual sign' of the period between Easter and the Parousia.[2] The firstfruits of the Gentiles are signs, an earnest of the fulfilment, foretastes of the final consummation. Just as justification, the gift of the Spirit,

---

[1] Cf. J. Jeremias, *The Parables of Jesus*[2], pp. 146–60.
[2] S. Knak, 'Neutestamentliche Missionstexte nach neuerer Exegese', in *Theologia Viatorum* V, 1954, p. 48.

sonship, the communion of the Lord's Table, are God's gracious gifts for the period of waiting for the consummation, so too are the Gentiles whom God brings into the Church of Jesus Christ. *The missionary task is a part of the final fulfilment*, a divine factual demonstration of the exaltation of the Son of Man, an *eschatology in process of realization*. It offers the possibility of co-operating with God in his gracious anticipation of the decisive hour of redemption described in Isa. 25: the Gentiles accepted as guests at God's Table (v. 6), the veil torn from their eyes (v. 7), and death abolished for ever (v. 8).

BIBLIOGRAPHY

S. AALEN *Die Begriffe 'Licht' und 'Finsternis' im AT, im Spätjudentum und im Rabbinismus* (= Skrifter utg. av Det Norske Videnskaps-Akademi i Oslo, Hist.-Filos. Kl. 1951 No. 1), Oslo 1951.

A. ALT 'Die Stätten des Wirkens Jesu in Galiläa territorialgeschichtlich betrachtet', Beiträge zur bibl. Landes- und Altertumskunde=*Zeitschrift des Deutschen Palästina-Vereins* 68, 1951, pp. 15–72, reprinted in *Kleine Schriften zur Geschichte des Volkes Israel* II, Munich 1953, pp. 436–55.

K. AXENFELD 'Die jüdische Propaganda als Vorläuferin und Wegbereiterin der urchristlichen Mission', *Missionswissenschaftliche Studien* (Festschrift für G. Warneck), Berlin 1904, pp. 1–80.

B. J. BAMBERGER *Proselytism in the Talmudic Period*, Cincinnati 1939.

A. BERTHOLET *Die Stellung der Israeliten und der Juden zu den Fremden*, Freiburg 1896.

S. BIALOBLOCKI *Die Beziehungen des Judentums zu Proselyten und Proselytismus*, Berlin 1930.

(H. L. STRACK AND) P. BILLERBECK *Kommentar zum NT aus Talmud und Midrasch*, Munich 1922–61, especially I pp. 102 ff., 354ff., 924 ff.; II pp. 715 ff.; III pp. 63, 139–55, 930; IV pp. 358 ff., 1063, 1066 f., 1117, 1174 ff.

K. BORNHÄUSER *Wollte Jesus die Heidenmission?*, Gütersloh 1903.

D. BOSCH *Die Heidenmission in der Zukunftsschau Jesu* (= Abhandlungen zur Theologie des Alten und Neuen Testaments 36), Zurich 1959.

W. G. BRAUDE *Jewish Proselyting in the First Five Centuries of the Common Era* (=Brown University Studies 6), Providence (R.I.) 1940.

A. COLE *The New Temple*, London 1950.

P. DALBERT *Die Theologie der hellenistisch-jüdischen Missionsliteratur unter Ausschluss von Philo und Josephus* (=Theol. Forschung 4), Hamburg-Volksdorf 1954.

Bibliography

F. M. DERWACTER *Preparing the Way for Paul, The Proselyte Movement in Later Judaism*, New York 1930.

J. DUPONT 'Le salut des Gentils et la signification du livre des Actes', *New Testament Studies* 6, 1959–60, pp. 132–56.

W. FREYTAG 'Mission im Blick aufs Ende', *EMZ* 3, 1942, pp. 321 ff.

A. FRIDRICHSEN *Der nedbrutna skiljemuren*, Uppsala 1954.

M. GOGUEL 'Jésus et les origines de l'universalisme chrétien', *RHPR* 12, 1932, pp. 193–211.

F. HAHN *Mission in the New Testament* (Studies in Biblical Theology 47), London 1965.

A. VON HARNACK *The Mission and Expansion of Christianity in the first three Centuries*, tr. and ed. J. Moffatt, London 1908.

K. HARTENSTEIN *Die Mission als theologisches Problem*, Berlin 1933.

J. HEMPEL 'Die Wurzeln des Missionswillens im Glauben des AT', *ZATW* 66, 1954, pp. 244–72.

J. JEREMIAS 'The Gentile World in the Thought of Jesus', *Studiorum Novi Testamenti Societas*, Bulletin III, 1952, reprinted 1963, pp. 18–28.

J. JEREMIAS *Jerusalem zur Zeit Jesu* IIB, Göttingen 1937, pp. 191–207 = [3]1962, pp. 354–70 (Die Proselyten).

J. JUSTER *Les Juifs dans l'empire romain* I, Paris 1914, pp. 253 ff.

M. KÄHLER 'Der Menschensohn und seine Sendung an die Menschheit', *Allgemeine Missions-Zeitschrift* 20, 1893, pp. 149–78.

G. D. KILPATRICK 'The Gentile Mission in Mark and Mark 13.9–11', *Studies in the Gospels, Essays in Memory of R. H. Lightfoot*, Oxford 1955, pp. 145–58.

S. KNAK 'Neutestamentliche Missionstexte nach neuerer Exegese', *Theologia Viatorum* V, 1954, pp. 27–50.

K. G. KUHN 'Das Problem der Mission in der Urchristenheit', *EMZ* 11, 1954, pp. 161–8.

K. LAKE 'Proselytes and God-fearers', *The Beginnings of Christianity* I 5, ed. K. Lake and H. J. Cadbury, London 1933, pp. 74–96.

L. LEGRAND 'Was Jesus Mission-Minded?', *Indian Ecclesiastical Studies* 3, 1964, pp. 87–104, 190–207.

J. LEIPOLDT *Jesu Verhältnis zu Griechen und Juden*, Leipzig 1941.

E. LERLE *Proselytenwerbung und Urchristentum*, Berlin 1960.

R. LIECHTENHAN *Die urchristliche Mission, Voraussetzungen, Motive und Methoden* (=Abhandlungen zur Theologie des Alten und Neuen Testaments 9), Zürich 1946.

E. LOHMEYER ' "Mir ist gegeben alle Gewalt!" Eine Exegese von Matt. 28.16–20', *In memoriam Ernst Lohmeyer*, ed. W. Schmauch, Stuttgart 1951, pp. 22–49.

M. LÖHR *Der Missionsgedanke im AT*, Freiburg-Leipzig 1896.

T. W. MANSON *Jesus and the Non-Jews*, London 1955.

M. MEINERTZ *Jesus und die Heidenmission* (=Neutestamentliche Abhandlungen I 1–2), Münster 1908, ²1925.

M. MEINERTZ *Wie Jesus die Mission wollte* (=Aschendorffs zeitgemässe Schriften 10), Münster 1926.

O. MICHEL 'Freudenbotschaft und Völkerwelt', *DT* 6, 1939, pp. 45–68.

O. MICHEL 'Gottesherrschaft und Völkerwelt', *EMZ* 2, 1941, pp. 225–32.

O. MICHEL 'Menschensohn und Völkerwelt', ibid. pp. 257–67.

O. MICHEL 'Der Abschluss des Matthäusevangeliums', *Ev. Th.* 10, 1950-51, pp. 16–26.

G. F. MOORE *Judaism in the First Three Centuries of the Christian Era*, Cambridge (Mass.) 1927–30, I pp. 229, 323–53, 432–4; III pp. 107–14.

J. MUNCK *Paul and the Salvation of Mankind*, London 1959.

A. OEPKE 'Internationalismus, Rasse und Weltmission im Lichte Jesu', *ZST* 10, 1932, pp. 278–300.

K. H. RENGSTORF *Die Mission unter den Heiden im Lichte des NT*, Hermannsburg 1936.

G. ROSEN, F. ROSEN AND G. BERTRAM *Juden und Phönizier, Das antike Judentum als Missionsreligion und die Entstehung der jüdischen Diaspora*, Tübingen 1929, pp. 62 ff.

G. ROSENKRANZ *Weltmission und Weltende* (=Beiträge zur Missionswissenschaft und evangelischen Religionskunde 2), Gütersloh 1951.

H. H. ROWLEY *The Missionary Message of the Old Testament*, London 1945.

H. SCHLIER 'Die Entscheidung für die Heidenmission in der Urchristenheit', *EMZ* 3, 1942, pp. 166–82, 208–12.

H. SCHMÖKEL *Jahwe und die Fremdvölker* (=Breslauer Studien zur Theologie und Religionsgeschichte 1), Breslau 1934.

G. SCHRENK *Die Weissagung über Israel im NT*, Zürich 1951.

E. SCHÜRER *Geschichte des jüdischen Volkes im Zeitalter Jesu Christi* III,[4] Leipzig 1909, pp. 150–88 (V. Die Proselyten).

A. SCHWEITZER *The Mysticism of Paul the Apostle*, London 1931, pp. 176 ff.

E. SELLIN 'Der Missionsgedanke im AT', *Neue allgemeine Missions-Zeitschrift* 2, 1925, pp. 33–45, 66–72.

M. SIMON *Verus Israel, Étude sur les relations entre chrétiens et juifs dans l'empire romain (135–425)*, Paris 1948, pp. 315–55.

E. SJÖBERG *Gott und die Sünder im palästinischen Judentum* (=Beiträge zur Wissenschaft vom Alten und Neuen Testament IV 27), Stuttgart 1938.

F. SPITTA *Jesus und die Heidenmission*, Giessen 1909.

W. STAERK 'Ursprung und Grenzen der Missionskraft der alttestamentlichen Religion', *TB* 4, 1925, pp. 25–37.

G. STÄHLIN 'Die Endschau Jesu und die Heidenmission', *EMZ* 7, 1950, pp. 97–105, 134–47.

H. STOEVESANDT *Jesus und die Heidenmission*, Diss. Göttingen 1943. Summary in *TLZ* 74, 1949, col. 242.

B. SUNDKLER 'Jésus et les païens', *RHPR* 16, 1936, pp. 462 ff., reprinted in *Arbeiten und Mitteilungen aus dem neutestamentlichen Seminar zu Uppsala* 6, Uppsala 1937, pp. 1–38.

F. WEBER *System der altsynagogalen palästinischen Theologie*, Leipzig 1880, pp. 64–78; [2]1897, pp. 65–79.

INDEX OF AUTHORS